*Urban Heroes, Volume 3: Stories of Ordinary Pittsburgh Residents Who Do Extraordinary Things*
by John W. Stanko and Karla Threadgill Byrd


ISBN 978-1-63360-020-1
For Worldwide Distribution
Printed in the U.S.A.

Urban Press
P.O. Box 8882
Pittsburgh, PA 15221-0882
412.646.2780

# Urban Heroes 2015

# INTRODUCTION

Geneva College at the Center for Urban Biblical Ministry serves non-traditional students. What do we mean by "non-traditional"? Our students are not your "typical" just-out-of-high-school variety, but usually come back to school after some life experience – sometimes a lot of life experience. We have students enroll who are in their 40s, some in their 50s and some who are even in their 60s! These students often helped put their children, grandchildren, nieces, nephews, neighbor kids and church youth through school. Then one day they decided, "Hey, it's my turn" and off to school they went. As you can tell, these are not ordinary or typical students, thus the term "nontraditional."

CUBM tries to provide all the support these students need, some of whom have been away from the books for forty years. During the course of counseling these students, we would hear the life stories of these students and would say to one another, "Their stories need to be published so others can be encouraged to do things later in life!' After saying this for many years, we started to strategize how this could be done.

We knew there are thousands of people who serve in our community day-in and day-out, who receive no recognition. They make no headlines, they seek no glory, they usually do not seek political office. They go to work, serve the poor, build their churches, raise their families and keep others from making new for the wrong reasons. Their efforts are truly heroic and they are happy to serve incognito. We thought their stories needed to be publicized, and they needed to be honored as the true heroes of our community.

We would often refer to our students as silent

heroes, which then led to us calling them urban heroes, since most of them were lifelong residents of the City of Pittsburgh. Then we had a writing class for students that sought to equip our students to write their own stories. While that idea did not pan out, we kept talking and brainstorming.

Then we decided not to limit the urban heroes' idea to our CUBM students, but to expand the effort to identify other worthy urban residents who had inspirational stories to tell. Finally, we landed on the concept for this project called *Urban Heroes: Stories of Ordinary Pittsburghers Who Do Extraordinary Things.* A grant from the Multicultural Arts Initiative helped get the ball rolling in 2010 and this Volume 3 represents the third class of honorees.

We put out the word for our first "class" of Heroes and twenty applications came in, all of which were accepted into the Program. The second class had 18 and now this year's class includes 15 worthy representatives. We are pleased that 53 people, some who are our students, have been recognized by us and others as heroes. As usual, their interview is included in this book, on the Pittsburgh Urban Heroes website and on our blog talk radio show, Urban Heroes.

Our first book contained only an excerpt of our interview, but this book contains the entire interview. We felt you, the readers, were being shortchanged by only seeing part of what the Heroes had to say. We know you will be inspired by their stories of family, sacrifice and hard work, and will endeavor to be an Urban Hero in your own way.

We do have one other small ulterior motive, however. If you fit the category of a nontraditional student that we mentioned above, then why not consider joining our other heroes here at the Center for Urban Biblical Ministry? Our vision is to see children, grandchildren, parents and grandparents all sitting in the same classroom, learning from the instructor and from one another. That family setting can only help to nurture a new generation of Urban Heroes whose stories are yet to be written.

We hope you enjoy this third edition of *Urban Heroes: Ordinary Pittsburghers Who Do Extraordinary Things*. Feel free to nominate your own heroes for inclusion in future book. You can do that by going to our website at www.pittsburghurbanheroes.com. Most importantly, get about the business of being a Hero yourself. Your community needs you and what's more, it's a rewarding way to live as you will see as you read the stories of the 2015 class of CUBM Urban Heroes.

Karla Threadgill Byrd
Dr. John Stanko
CUBM Executive Director
Urban Heroes Project Coordinator

[illegible]

URBAN HERO

# DR. TODD ALLEN

*Todd Allen is a part-time CUBM faculty member who teaches History of the Civil Rights Movement and Speech. He is a full-time professor at Grove City College in the Communications Department. Todd is also founder of The Common Ground Project, an organization which, among other things, sponsors an annual Retracing the Steps of Civil Rights Tour. Both Mrs. Byrd and Dr. Stanko have been on the tour. They started Todd's interview by asking the status of the 2015 Tour.*

**JS: How is the tour shaping up this year?**

TA: The tour is shaping up well. We're a little smaller with about 25 people this year. But I tell people whether we have 50 or 5, we will have a blessed experience.

**JS: How many years is this for you, Dr. Allen?**

TA: This will be year fourteen.

**KB: Are there any special celebrations this year?**

TA: This year is the 50th anniversary of the events in Selma, and there were many activities there recently, and they will continue to have special programming throughout 2015. We are also hoping to have a few events along the way as we travel. It's too early to say whether that will happen, but there is always a surprise or two up our sleeve.

**JS: Mrs. Byrd, when you think of Dr. Allen, why do you believe he was nominated and is qualified as an Urban Hero?**

**KB: Todd and I – I call him Todd because we have known each**

**other for some time – met on campus at Geneva College. He also managed the site we had at Aliquippa and he has been a teacher at the CUBM campus for some time. This is a young man who has gone through the ranks of education. He earned his undergraduate and graduate degree and I was so pleased when he received his PhD from Duquesne. He has a great family, and the tour is a family project and is amazing. The entire family is involved. His mother comes, his sisters, and their children. This is how we should do business to pass it on and how to live a Christian life. And Todd and his family are a good example of that. We were pleased to nominate him to be an Urban Hero.**

TA: I am humbled to have been nominated. I just love the fact that she continually calls me a young man.

**JS: Karla talked about family. Fill us in on Todd Allen. Where were you born and tell us about your family? Bring us up to speed on who you are.**

TA: I'm a native of Western Pennsylvania; Beaver Falls to be exact. I grew up here and continued to live and raise my family here. I am one of six children. I'm in the middle. My parents are Caperse and Wilma Allen. My father passed a few years ago but my mother is still with us. I would like to say I married my high school sweetheart, but truth be told, in high school she wouldn't give me the time of day. But we have been married for 21 years. We have a 15-year-old son in high school. I have been blessed to not only go to school in the region, but to find employment in the region starting with Geneva College. Currently I am with Grove City College.

**JS: What did you study in school? And why?**

TA: I began my undergraduate career at Morehouse College in Atlanta. I had an amazing African American history teacher in high school, and one of the people she focused on was Dr. King, because this was the time when Dr. King's birthday became a national holiday. I was determined to go to school where he went to school, which was Morehouse. I had a great experience there my freshman year, but you never know what God has in store. Lo and behold, I transferred to a place I said I would never go, back to my hometown of Beaver Falls and Geneva College from where I graduated in 1991. I started out after graduation working in admissions and student life. My degrees are actually in communication and rhetorical studies. So for the past 17 or 18 years, I have taught in the discipline of communication studies.

**JS: What are you teaching at Grove City College now?**

TA: In 2014 I was invited to the campus at Grove City to speak in chapel for the Martin Luther King holiday. Apparently I must have given a message that was well received because within a month I was contacted by the college and encouraged to apply for a position they had. Within weeks of that call, I interviewed and was hired. It's been a smooth transition and I have been blessed. Again, another one of those chapters in life that I never saw coming but, lo and behold, that is where God ends up sending you.

**KB: Do you want to tell us a little bit about your community focus? What are you doing in the community?**

TA: I have been an elected member of the Big Beaver School Board for 15 years. I am currently up for re-election this year. I am going for my fifth term, which will probably be my final term since that will be 20 years, and that's enough to have done any one thing. But again, I am blessed because I work in the field of education and here in my hometown, there was an opportunity 15 years ago to run for office. Sometimes people will sit back and complain about things, but no one wants to step in and work to address those problems a community has. It's not all peaches and cream when you are a school board member, but I've been blessed to give back to my community by serving in that way.

We also mentioned the Civil Rights Tour, it is something that is open to whosoever wants to go and we draw people from all over the country. I am quite proud of the fact that it's something that comes out of little old Western Pennsylvania in a place called Beaver Falls that is touching so many people.

I'm a member of Second Baptist Church in Beaver Falls, the church I grew up in as a child. I remain actively involved in that congregation, but I am also supporting others who have come along. There is a great group of young people now who are rising up doing community programming in their own way in that church. I'm at that age now where I still look forward to those who are older who continue to mentor me, but now I also have the responsibility to mentor those who are coming along and know when to get out of the way and be led by this younger group. That is so important if we are to have a vibrant future.

**JS: Jesus said a prophet is not without honor, except in his own hometown. How tough has it been? It sounds like God has given you favor. Any drawbacks to being in the church you grew up in and being on the school board? Your son is in the school district. What's it like ministering and working so much in your hometown?**

TA: I laughed initially at your question because I have a saying that everybody who stands up and claps is not necessarily giving you a standing ovation. Some people are just using that moment as an opportunity to stretch. I have people who are very supportive of me and affirm me and the work I do and that feels good. But you're always going to have the doubters and your haters. I don't get too excited when someone praises me and I don't get too disappointed when someone criticizes me. I just try to get up every day and do what's right the best I can and try to do it better tomorrow.

**KB: What's the website for the Common Ground Tour?**

TA: There isn't a website, but there is a Facebook page, and it's called Returning to the Roots of Civil Rights Tour https://www.facebook.com/pages/Returning-To-The-Roots-Of-Civil-Rights-Tour/. Periodically throughout the year, we also conduct various programming. In 2015, a lot of that programming happened at the front end of the year. We sponsored a community forum in Beaver Falls on relationships between communities and law enforcement. We brought in nationally-known documentary filmmaker Keith Beauchamp for that program. We've had Rutha Harris, one of the original SNCC Freedom Singers, as well as LPGA tour member Renee Powell from Clearview Golf Course in East Canton come speak in the area. We'll be doing some small programs after June once the tour is out of the way. Come fall we will probably move into a film series. But people can keep up to date if they "like" our Facebook page. Through that we will let them know when we have some events going on.

**KB: One of the things people don't realize is there is an African-American-owned golf course within driving distance of Pittsburgh.**

TA: Yes, in East Canton, Ohio. I'm glad you brought that up. We call our tour *Returning to the Roots of Civil Rights* for a reason. We could go all over this country if we wanted to visit sites of the Civil Rights Movement, but we intentionally go south and even when we go south, we don't go everywhere we could possibly go. As the veterans of the Movement remind me, we don't spend near enough time in every town and city as we could or should. But the Tour is an opportunity to introduce people to the landmark sites and moments of the Movement. When people return to whatever community they came from, they can explore the history of civil rights in their respective communities. I hope people go back home and look at the current issues and challenges going on to get involved in addressing those. I tell people if they go on the trip, and all they do is take a lot of nice pictures and buy some t-shirts and the souvenir mug, they've missed it. The Tour is about continuing to make a difference in their community once they get home.

**JS: Todd as we get older we get a little more reflective. What were your most significant accomplishments? What do you look back at and reflect on now and think you were really glad you were involved in or did that?**

TA: This might sound a little sappy, but honestly when I look at my son, I enjoy watching the man he is becoming. It lets me know the man that raised me, and the others, did something right and something that stuck. And that I am in the process of doing something right - not perfect, but doing something right. The trips are great, the people I have met are great, the awards and accolades are great, but watching my son is the most meaningful.

**KB: And I would agree with you, and that's why I pointed out that your family is involved in it. Because this is how children really do learn to work and study and be successful.**

TA: He is 15 now and has been traveling on the tour with me since he was five. I honestly tell people he could do it without me. I fear the one day he comes to me and says, "Dad, you know what? You're fired." Maybe when that day comes I can just fly into certain cities and let him run everything else. I say that jokingly, but I look forward to the day that he and some of the other younger people who have gone on this experience launch their own trips. It's about getting the message out by any means, and so I am excited people are inspired to go forward.

**JS: What do you do to grow? What inputs do you have in your life? Reading? Studying? Authors? What do you do to stay sharp mentally and intellectually and on the cutting edge?**

TA: Well, I've never met a book store I don't like. I constantly have books stacked by my bed and favorite chair in my office. I am always looking at something. That can run the gamut from a book on history to something on sports to something more motivational or inspirational. It just kind of depends. I also like circling myself with a lot of good friends who are like-minded. I look forward to those conversations we have formally and informally. Golf is a good walk spoiled, but there is something to be said for getting out there when it's nice and warm and sunny, it's just you and a golf club and a ball and a couple of buddies. I think all of those in differing ways help to keep me sharp.

**JS: So that's why you stop in Clearview? You probably get some passes. Tell the truth now. Do they invite you back and do you play there?**

TA: Oh I play there quite a bit. I tell people I owe it to Clearview to play there a couple times a year. Because of a course like Clearview, I can go to just about any other course my money can get me into as a person of color.

**KB: What advice would you want to give someone who wants to follow your path?**

TA: Honestly, I don't think it's about following my path. I think it's about following the path the Lord has set for you. The thing I tell my college students all the time is the key to be faithful in the moment. You can't worry about what's going to happen a year, two years, or five years from now. It's that faithfulness you have in the moment that is most important, doing the work set before you that can open up those doors of opportunity down the road, sometimes when you least expect it. The last thing I tell people is to never say never. I have repeatedly said never, that I would never go back to Geneva or go to Grove City, and finding that when God is sending you somewhere, He is going to send you over that "never."

He isn't going to send you to a place He hasn't prepared for you to be.

**JS: In the realm of communications and in teaching, in your settings has publishing and broadcasting or issue or something that has been required of you? Have you done it? Or do you see that in your future?**

TA: My undergraduate degree was in broadcast communication. I used to say my mother was going to see me on the news in a good way. I've never done that as a profession, but as a result of a number of activities, including the Tour, I have had opportunities in both radio and television and that's been exciting. As far as publishing, I am part of a very exciting project with a young scholar out of New York. Dr. Anthony Bradley brought together a group of African American Christian academics from a variety of Christian colleges and range of disciplines to contribute to an edited book called *Black Scholars in White Space: New Vistas in the African American Christian Academy*. That's an opportunity for me to share the work I am doing in civil rights and write a reflective piece on the importance of memory. that's been my most recent project.

Of course I am constantly preparing for conference presentations throughout the year. I have a big one I am waiting to hear on that goes back to the idea of law enforcement and community relations, particularly in light of a range of events that have happened over the past year or so. And honestly I look at what I do every day walking into the classroom. I have a crisis communication course to attend after this interview where we wrestle with difficult issues of individuals or organizations and how to handle those.

It's always exciting to sit down with these students. Sometimes when we are talking about figures from history, I ask the students how old they were when something happened, and I know the answer is they were one or two years old. It's so comical to me, because I look back and remember it like it was yesterday, and for them they weren't even here or just got here. They also introduce me to some of the more recent events of their generation and era, so it's a nice give and take.

**KB: I think about my life and what's happening now is what happened at the beginning of the Civil Rights Movement with the riots, protests and things like that. The Common Ground Tour shows people we can't forget where we have come from and the need to keep moving forward. I want to voice my concern with all these things happening concerning police brutality and community violence.**

TA: You are absolutely right. One theme emphasized in the Tour is that the struggle continues. It takes on different forms, but freedom is a constant struggle.

**JS: With Urban Press I have two things we are working on. One is Millie Johnson's dissertation from Regent on ethics in law enforcement. I have a priest friend who teaches at William & Mary who did something on ethics in law enforcement and he is working on his PhD at Oxford and I thought this thing is going to read like eating sawdust, but It's really excellent. We're looking at how he can publish both of those treatises because they are so timely. They are biblically based, and relevant for what is going on. Certainly what we hope to do with Urban Press is to put material out there that can somehow contribute to the issues of the day. The brutality along with the institutional and personal racism in some of our systems are some things we have to continue to war against. What's the racial mix of those on the tour?**

TA: It's funny because that's a question I am often asked and there's an assumption people make that the majority will be black. Honestly, the 2015 will have more white people than black. Usually my numbers are about 50/50. As Karla mentioned, if you take out my family then it's typically more white than black. I emphasize to people that, as my pastor often says, the tour is open to whosoever will. But the Tour does not focus on black history. it's American history and world history. It's the story of God's hand in history. The last time I checked that's for everyone.

**JS: I would imagine that African Americans would feel that they lived this. White folk, like me, we're sometimes out to lunch, but we're catching up. We don't want to be trendy or chic, because we can't fully enter into what people of color went through in those eras, but we can certainly strive to understand it better. I had to ask myself what I would have done if I was alive when Martin Luther King, Jr. was in his prime, and I probably would have done nothing. But that's not really the right question. The question is what can I do now?**

TA: I was going to say that. It's the question. What am I doing right now? What are the contemporary issues that are crying out for people of faith to engage?

**KB: What are your future plans, Todd?**

TA: For me, it's about being faithful in the present. I am enjoying teaching. I would like to, as I get a little older, transfer over to something more administrative, continuing to keep my foot in the classroom, but also doing some more administrative kind of work. I am a strong advocate of reconciliation. I could see myself working on some level systematically as well as individually to help our colleges and universities come to grips with what it means to be the beloved community, as Dr. King referred to us. That's something I have my eye on towards the future. What that means in terms of where, I am open to see what happens. Short-term future, however, is that I have a stack of papers to grade!

**JS: You mentioned your high school teacher and you mentioned the church. Talk to us about any other people who influenced what you are doing today? Or maybe just expand on your high school teacher and what it was that impacted you so much that directed and shaped the course of your life.**

TA: There are so many people and it's like an award show where you get in trouble when you start naming names. But really, it begins at home with my mom and dad and what they modeled for me in terms of their relationship and love for one another. It was also their expectations of me and their love for me and encouragement and support so that whenever I stepped foot outside that door, I knew that at least two people had my back. And obviously it's so important that when we send our children to school, we have teachers who value, respect and challenge them.

I was raised in an era where parents and teachers knew each other quite well and were often friends outside of their respective areas of responsibility. That's what the teacher you mentioned was for me. Her name was Mrs. Paulette Potter and I had her in junior high. I will never forget in ninth grade when she asked what my future plans were, and I said college. She asked how I was going to get there and I said a basketball scholarship. she asked what I would do if I got hurt, and I looked at her as a 14-year-old and asked what she was talking about because we don't get hurt. She warned I had better have a backup plan.

I had never considered until that moment that I needed a backup plan and of course her backup plan was academics. I had been a good student, good enough to stay out of trouble at home, but not so good that I received academic accolades, because at the time I didn't think that was the cool thing to do. Mrs. Potter really pressed me in ninth grade. And I took on her challenge and did a variety of things.

She was the one who encouraged me to run for class offices, and the more I became involved in the life of the school, leadership and various other academic opportunities, things really took off for me. She was the one who in a more systematic way introduced me to African American history and culture. and that lit a fire that has stayed with me. It was really powerful.

The very first year I did the Tour, she was one of the participants to go on it because she had been someone I approached with the idea. She encouraged me, as expected, to follow through. I remember watching as she was meeting some of the veterans of the Civil Rights Movement. She told them that never could she have imagined one of her students would take her to the places to meet the people she taught him about.

For me as an educator, that was profound to hear my former teacher say something like that. Truth be told, one of the reasons I am still doing the tour is one of my former student saw something I did in that first trip and was able to secure some funding for that dream to grow into what I have done for the last 14 years. Mrs. Potter was phenomenal.

Obviously the church has impacted me, being surrounded by people who knew me before I knew me has been a blessing. Over the years a lot of those folks have been transitioning on to glory. Yet to have a church that when you step out into a community has your back and supports you, means a lot to moving forward. One of the things in life is I realize I'm not perfect, but I don't want to let those people down. I have long lived by that credo that service is the price we pay for the space we occupy. There have been generations before me that opened doors for me and I can do no less than continue to open doors for those that are coming behind me.

**JS: We did one Urban Hero interview and that person had gone to Seton Hill. She said when her mother was driving up the hill to the school for her freshman year, the mom told her that a lot of people worked to make it possible for her to go to school, and not to mess it up. She said it was the first time she felt the**

**weight of so many people who had gone before her, and she said she received that and did not screw it up. I'll never forget that interview and her mother's simple words saying she wasn't going up that hill alone. In the same manner, you're not going on the tour alone and Mrs. Byrd doesn't do what she does alone. It's a lot of people going along with you. And may we always remember that. Do you have a favorite book? Favorite movie?**

TA: Favorite book. I don't think I could limit it to just one. I hate to give it the answer so many artists give, but the next one is my favorite. Favorite movie? My niece and I will watch *The Color Purple* every time it comes on as if we've never seen it before. We love just quoting it back and forth to each other. I have no idea why.

**JS: What did you think of the movie *Selma* that came out earlier this year? Did you think it was an accurate description? Were you pleased?**

TA: I was pleased. I did have to take my historian hat off as there were things that were and weren't accurate about the film. It told a powerful story that holds the potential to introduce people to a chapter in history that otherwise they would not know about. It might spur them on to go read some of the more accurate or detailed historical accounts of what went on there, or maybe even to visit Selma. There are a number of people, and it's shocking to me, who have never heard of Bloody Sunday. Who didn't know about the Selma to Montgomery March? But when the film came out and was so well publicized and promoted, that encouraged people to travel to Selma. Once you have gone to these places where history has happened, you can't be the same. So if the movie has the potential to do that, then I say kudos, it's a great film. We'll be watching that aboard the bus. We use that bus as our rolling classroom and that will be one of the films we will see, hopefully prior to getting into Selma. So it's something I will continue to use in the classroom, but will also supplement it and fill in the gaps as they say.

**KB: To me it was so significant, because I remember the Freedom Riders. So as we were riding the bus I was saying this is what it must have felt like. I think it was the perfect vehicle. In fact, my sister came from Philadelphia last year to attend and she is still talking about it.**

TA: I encourage people to journal about their experience. I remember vividly when I went on my first tour prior to leading trips of my own. That was one of the things I chronicled in my journal that as we are traveling, this is reminiscent in some ways, at least the destination we were going to, to what folks did on the Freedom Rides. What was so different was I didn't have to worry about where I was going to lay my head at night. I didn't have to worry where I was going to get something to eat or where to use the restroom facilities or anything like that.

I was blessed to be in Selma back in March when the President and First Lady arrived. To me one of the most powerful moments of that entire weekend was watching that motorcade, fifty years almost to the minute, come across that bridge. Knowing fifty years prior John Lewis were being beaten nearly to death, and fifty years later, here comes, I don't want to say the fulfillment of that dream, but as they said, one down payment on it. John Lewis himself said if you had told him fifty years ago as he was being beaten that he would be back at this bridge introducing the first African American president, he would have called you crazy. My goodness, look at what God has done in that time. Even though we continue to have work to do. But look at what has been accomplished.

**JS: Do you have a favorite passage or Bible verse?**

TA: Micah 6:8: "He has shown you, oh man, what is good, and what does the Lord require of you but to do justice, love mercy, and walk humbly with God." Honestly, that is what I attempt to do every day. Some days are better than others, but that is what I attempt to do every day.

**KB: I want to say for those of us who lived through the Civil Right's Movement that it's really a cathartic thing going back and seeing it. Because at least for me, it was a life experience. Every day coming home, the riots were going on, Martin Luther King getting shot. I was college at that point and was thinking I needed to get out of there and go home. To see what people have done and that it's such a difference in the South than in the North and how they have used the experiences to move on. It was healing for me and my sister had the same experience.**

TA: That's one of the things we've been blessed with. Not only do folk come from a variety of geographic and ethnic backgrounds, but from quite a spread of ages. Our youngest is eight and I'm not allowed to say how old our oldest is, and every stage in between. As the two of you were sharing, we have had participants who were around when a lot of these key moments happened and can remember where they were. And for others, this is just black and white footage they have seen in documentary films. There is something about the experience, whether you were around or not, that has a way of bringing together that diverse age range of participants we are blessed to have.

**JS: Thank you for making this experience available to us.**

# OLIVER BYRD

*Oliver Byrd retired a few years ago after a long career with Bank of New York Mellon, but not before he made a deep impact on the Pittsburgh community. He spearheaded the effort to build the August Wilson Center after having served as United Way Chairman in Allegheny County. He is the husband of Urban Hero Karla Threadgill Byrd, and serves on the faculty at the Center for Urban Biblical Ministry, teaching math and business subjects.*

**KB: Our next Urban Hero is someone I have known very well. I've known him for years! He is a Christian and a devoted family man with two wonderful daughters and a grandson. He grew up in the Pittsburgh area where he attended Westinghouse High School, went on to Harvard, worked for IBM, and returned to Pittsburgh to do his life work in the city. He has done all that and is now retired and enjoying himself. And this Urban Hero is Oliver Wendell Byrd, my husband.**

**JS: Thank you. Karla gave a thumbnail sketch about you. Tell us about growing up, where you went to college, and then we'll go back to fill in the gaps.**

OB: I am a Pittsburgh native and grew up in the Homewood Brushton section of Pittsburgh. I attended the Baxter Elementary School and went on to attend Westinghouse High School. Westinghouse is probably the place where I got a lot of my grounding. I was president of the student body there, captain of the chess team, and first trumpet and first chair in both the orchestra and the band. I really enjoyed the experience of meeting and getting to know people there. At that time, high school went from 7th grade through 12th grade, so you really had a good opportunity to establish a lot of relationships.

From there I went to Harvard University on a scholarship, and majored in math and social psychology. While I was there, at the age of 19, I had an opportunity to work at the NASA electronic research center in Cambridge and was exposed to some of the greatest scientists in the world. At that time, we were still working on lunar landing modules and things of that nature and it proved to be a great experience. It was also a time that was pretty troubling in our country. During the time I was at Harvard, we saw the assassination of Dr. Martin Luther King, Jr. and Bobby Kennedy and a number of things that caused campus unrest. The Vietnam War was still going on. I saw both the greatest one could see in terms of academic pursuits as well as a lens on the real world we all live in, and that we were all going to come to be leaders in at some point in time.

After graduating from Harvard, I worked with IBM corporation as a systems engineer in Cambridge, Massachusetts. I did that for two or three years and decided it was time to come back to Pittsburgh. I came back and achieved a master's in business administration from the University of Pittsburgh's Katz Graduate School of Business and began working in the area of community development, small business consulting, and things of that nature. My concentration in graduate school was finance and economics, with a minor in human behavior and organization. I have had a pretty long and varied educational career and travels, living not only in Pittsburgh, but also Boston and New York.

**JS: Before we go on to the next question, was it a dream Harvard? Or did it unfold later in your high school experience? Talk about how that came about.**

OB: It wasn't a dream, per se. Academic excellence was

always a requirement in my house and certainly in terms of my own values and goals. I did fairly well in high school and grade school. I guess I came to be recognized throughout the city as someone who had the potential to attend a school like Harvard. I hadn't thought about applying or anything, but I had a counselor at Westinghouse High School who many people will remember and have had an opportunity to interact with over the years. Her name was Dr. Helen Faison, and she is the one who really encouraged me to place an application to Harvard. She thought that academically I had the credentials to be accepted, though obviously it was a long shot. You didn't see very many African Americans at the Ivy League schools. And speaking of Dr. Helen Faison, she is someone who has followed me in my career, from the very early stages of my life.

**JS: So, important to have a mentor you think? Did that help you to become an Urban Hero?**

OB: I'm not sure what made me an Urban Hero, but I will say that is important to have people in your life who you can rely on, to go to and model your own behaviors after, whose values are ones you support, admire, and can adopt as your own. Back in those days, we didn't necessarily call it a mentor, but certainly Dr. Helen Faison did play that kind of a role for me, as did a number of other individuals who were attentive to the kinds of obstacles and opportunities presented to young African Americans at that time.

**JS: Talk to us a little bit about when I got to you know you at Mellon Bank, which is now Bank of New York/Mellon, which led you to quite a bit of community involvement. Talk to our readers about that aspect of your career.**

OB: When I think about my career, I think of it in two parts. One would be the vocation and the other would be the avocation. BNY/Mellon would be a good example of a vocation where my focus has always been problem solving, using advanced analytical techniques. I happened to pursue that through banking. I was an employee of the Bank of New York/Mellon for 35 years, before retiring not too long ago. That gave me an opportunity to volunteer in a number of different capacities here in this city. My avocation happens to be working with those who are under-represented, those who are disadvantaged, and using those skills or whatever talents I bring to bear on solving those kinds of problems. Specifically, my work has involved health and human services, along with the arts.

**JS: What were some of the aspects of some of the avocation that you got involved? I know there were significant ones.**

OB: I think the one that a lot of people would know about would be the 20 plus years I spent volunteering with the United Way of Allegheny County. I spent those years learning about the individual agencies and learning about the health and human service challenges that we face as a community. In that time, I spent 10 years as a vice chairman of the board in overseeing resource management. I completely revised the management review and enhancement system, which we eventually outsourced to Robert Morris College.

And at the same time, spent two years as its chairman of the board. I had a real opportunity to get a sense of the types of problems we face as a community, whether talking about race-related issues, societal issues which have to do health outcomes and the role of caregivers in that entire process. I got to know a lot of agency executives, a lot of the agencies themselves, as well as a number of recipients of United Way support. That was a very meaningful experience for me and really was consistent with the idea of working to help others who are in need of our support. Probably one of the more important accolades that came out of that was being named the United Way Volunteer of the Year in 1994 for my work in overseeing in fund distribution over the years. We distributed more than $35,000,000 in health and human services grants to United Way agencies over each of some 20 years.

My other avocation happens to be art and culture. And it's a love of mine going back to the days of being a trumpet player in an orchestra and the band, and even playing in a funk group back in my Westinghouse days. Arts and culture are incredibly important. In our community, when we think about quality of life, we can't think about it without including arts and culture as a way that people identify themselves, their roots, and their role in society.

I have spent a number of years, probably as many years in supporting arts and culture, as I've spent in health and human services. And as many years in arts and culture as I spent in the financial services arena. I'm probably known for my work with the Multi-Cultural Arts Initiative, which was a supporting organization of the Pittsburgh Foundation and the Heinz Endowment. Over a twenty-year time period, we raised and distributed about $7,000,000 in grants to various arts and cultural organizations, specifically African American arts organizations, in order to have that aspect of our society and that aspect of our artistic and cultural contributions be seen in the same way that those of the majority population are seen.

Beyond that, there was a passion for having a physical representation of African American art and culture, and I spent probably 12-15 years working on the development and building of the August Wilson Center for African American Arts and Culture. In that process, while they said we couldn't do it, we raised more than $35,000,000 specifically for the building and operation of the center. The total cost was $42,000,000, so we still had a ways to go, but certainly we raised more money for this particular project than for any other African-American project in the history of the region.

**JS: Congratulations, for it was just a wonderful effort. I know it's gotten politicized of late. In my mind, I'll never let it tarnish the efforts that you put in along with so many others. The Multi-Cultural Arts Initiative got the Urban Heroes program started. If you remember 2010 or 2011 as that was winding down, we got a $6,000 grant to produce the first volume of Urban Heroes. We had our celebration at the August Wilson Center. And it was a highlight for me of my involvement with CUBM and the community. We were the beneficiaries of your efforts there Oliver, and we want to thank you for that.**

**KB: The other thing we want to mention is because of that grant, we've started a publishing company so that African American people can tell their stories, share their thoughts and also their theology. Who influenced to do what you do?**

OB: It really was a number of people who influenced me. I'm a thief, in the best sense of the word. I look at the best characteristics of people I come into contact and steal from them, those elements of their personality and life's work I think would be useful in my own life. Therefore, I've looked at people like Dr. Helen Faison. I've been influenced by local people like Jim Roddey and Marty McGuinn, who was chairman and CEO of Bell & Bank Corporation. I've looked at people like Martin Luther King, Jr., and the sacrifices he made serving underserved communities and underrepresented individuals. I've looked at a number of people, high and low, as examples of the kind of person I wanted to be and as a way of seeing he path that I would ultimately take in life.

**JS: You mentioned Dr. King. Were there other authors or significant figures, not just contemporaries, but of the past whose lives you tried to emulate and whose values you incorporated into your work?**

OB: I can identify a number of people. Among those are people like Medgar Evers, who gave the ultimate sacrifice in trying to support those who were less fortunate in this society. I think about people in the arts and entertainment field who were blackballed during the McCarthy era who wanted simply to practice their craft, but were not able to do so because of a political view that suggested they were communists, or something of that nature. Again, I've been a thief, stealing from all of them.

More recently, the three influencers who have driven my own values and have anchored my own life work are, as I mentioned, Dr. Martin Luther King, Jr., who demonstrated to me that faith in God and concern for the oppressed amongst us, and the courage to face adversity were critically important.

Then there was a Dr. Herbert Simon, who most people don't know about. He was a professor at Carnegie Mellon University back in the '60s and early '70s. He is considered the father of artificial intelligence. Dr. Simon demonstrated a different approach to problem solving. He pursued excellence in everything he did, and demonstrated the importance of being rooted in a disciplined approach to problem solving in whatever role he was playing in society.

I have mentioned and need to continue to mention Dr. Helen Faison, because she has been a part of my life from its earliest stages. Her stature as a leader in our church helped me understand the concept of a leader as servant. Even with her incredible credentials professionally, it was her personal life example that impressed me most. Last, but not least, she was always encouraging me in everything that I did. Knowing that a person of her stature was following my every move, advising me to always tow the line and encouraging me to take measured risks in life, I could not do anything but be involved in the community. She had an involvement in so many organizations, because she was asked to be involved. She didn't have the time to do all those kinds of things, but she tried. And those were the kinds of behaviors and examples that have driven me in the direction I have taken in life. You just can't say no sometimes, even though you don't necessarily have time.

**JS: It's been said that If you want something done, give it to a busy person. The other thought I had was there is a book titled *Steal Like an Artist*. That book points out that all of us are impacted by things that we see and examples we have beheld. There's nothing wrong with assimilating the best of what we see and assimilating them into a life philosophy, which you have done so well. You mentioned church. You are still in the church you grew up in. Correct?**

OB: Baptist Temple Church was about three blocks from where I lived the first thirteen of my life, and I still attend there. It's an important community beacon of hope for Homewood Brushton and for Pittsburgh. I think it's important that we continue to work with community churches, not as opposed to, but in addition to, the mega churches that have come to be very popular these days. Baptist Temple Church in Homewood has been around since 1921, and personally I have had the opportunity to be a teacher in the Sunday School, the superintendent of Sunday School for seven years, and also the chairman of the board of trustees for about seven years. Today, I continue to serve as a trustee of the organization and the chair of its overall budget committee.

**KB: As we look toward the future, what are your plans?**

OB: Oh, I've always been more interested in the journey than the destination. A few of the guiding principles regarding my future are as follows. I want to let God use me in the ways that He would have me to serve; to try and be more active in supporting the Baptist Temple Church and my pastor there, Rev. Rodney Lyde; and to pass along my life lessons and experiences to the next generation of black leadership. I've been working with the church in terms of its property expansion and growth into the next century and that sort of thing.

I've also been trying to pass on the lessons learned from initiatives like the Multi-Cultural Arts Initiative and the United Way and the August Wilson Center, to those who came after me who are today's and tomorrow's new leaders. I'm looking forward to those kinds of activities as opposed to having a specific goal that I've set for myself. I enjoy teaching and research, so I will continue doing those kinds of things. I love being a consultant and will continue to consult.

**KB: As you're thinking about that, what advice would you have for someone wanting to follow in your footsteps?**

OB: I'm not sure I'd encourage anyone to follow in my footsteps. If anyone wanted to, however, I'd say there are six things that are guiding principles for them or the advice that I would give. One, I would say surround yourself with good people, especially people who are smarter than you are. There's no shame in having someone smarter than you around, because it's from them that you learn, and it's from them that you refine whatever direction it is you are headed in.

Two, don't believe those who tell you that something can't be done, merely because it's never been done before. If we thought that way, we'd never accomplish anything new. Three, stay humble. Over the course of a lifetime you get a lot of rewards and acknowledgements for the work that you do. Just as fast as you can go up, however, you can come down, because you become a target. Especially as an African American leader, you become a target of the system that tries to undermine its African American leadership in order that the system might be maintained. Make no mistake about it, my objective in life has been to change the system in a way that is beneficial to everyone.

Four, be open to learning new things. Even as you lead others in the way that they should go, you've got to keep learning, studying and stay at the leading edge of technology, health and human services issues, of our Christian thinking and things of that nature, world events, and economics in order to do your best work. Fifth, I would say maintain your integrity. And finally, strive for excellence in everything you do.

**JS: What have you been reading lately? What do you like to read? Do you have a reading strategy or philosophy?**

OB: I do, but it is clearly not something a lot of people would like to follow because I love reading technical publications. That includes things that have to do with artificial intelligence, or with futurism strategies for defining what our future is going to be, or techniques to discern those kinds of things as they trend. I love reading books that have to do with personal struggles people have overcome and become a good story for others - the ways that people have sacrificed and taken life's lemons and turned them into the preverbial lemonade. I love those kinds of books.

I like reading the Bible because as is true with many folks, the most important things I've learned in life I learned in Sunday School. The Bible really has taught me how to live my life and how to make decisions as I move through life and has helped form my own worldview.

I also enjoy the classics. I'm a big fan of Fyodor Dostoyevsky, who wrote *The Brothers Karamazov*. I'm a big fan of some of the authors who were prominent during the '60s and '70s, people like Arthur Miller and Edward Albee. I love the Greek classics, Aeneas and Agamemnon, and things of that genre. They can include strange kinds of things that are reflective of my reading philosophy of being eclectic. There is something we can learn from every discipline, and we shouldn't limit ourselves to merely one area of study or one area of reading in order to understand the world that we live in.

**JS: Apart from the Bible, which author impacted you the most?**

OB: I'm going to say that it was probably Langston Hughes, an African American author, noted for his work during the Harlem Renaissance years. His writing was reachable. It was accessible to the common man. And yet, it also contained lessons to be learned by the leadership, not only of this country, but of the world. I think Langston Hughes' work, in general, also stimulated the work of several other authors. I enjoy his work particularly, but I also enjoy the pure literary genius of someone like James Baldwin and some of the work he produced. I was also impressed by Frederick Douglas and his work. I could go on and on about authors who have influenced me with the work that they've done.

**KB: Let me see if I can guess this one. What's your favorite Bible verse?**

OB: "I can do all things through Christ who strengthens me," which is Philippians 4:13. That is my life verse, but we had others we said in Sunday School that guided my approach to studying the Bible. One of those is 2 Timothy 2:15, which says "Study to shew thyself approved unto God, a workman that needeth not to be ashamed, rightly dividing the word of truth." The importance of that is if you are going to be an advocate and disciple of Jesus Christ, you've got to know His word. You cannot know his word except that you study His word and correctly interpret His word or respond to questions about His word that are asked by those who are not saved.

And as the second part of that, for the Sunday School, "Go ye, therefore and teach all nations, baptizing them in the name of the Father, and of the Son, and of the Holy

Spirit," which is Matthew 28:19. That one was important because as a Sunday School student, as a Christian, if you ask the question what you should do, Jesus made it very clear through His disciples that He wanted them to go out and disciple – that He wanted them to go out and bring people to Him. They didn't have to do anything to get them saved. All they had to do was bring them to Him. That particular Sunday School verse was important in my life and in directing the Sunday School program in terms of new Christians coming to life in Christ.

**JS: Oliver, I'm sure you saw the movie *Selma*. Talk to us, not only about the movie, and what it represented for you in your life journey.**

OB: Selma was a very important piece of work. I saw it and it was disturbing and troubling, but at the same time it was very well done. It was a good representation of life as we understood it back in those days. I think one of the things it points out clearly is the importance of television in our society. Television made the Selma story available to the entire country so we could see the kinds of horrors that were being perpetrated on African Americans in the South, and indeed throughout the country. Not everyone knew that because information was limited.

One of the things that made Selma so personal for me is that in my sophomore year at Harvard, there was a classmate of mine whose name was Bobby Gaines who was from Alabama. He went home for the summer, as we all did, and while he was home in Alabama, he strayed into the wrong area and ended up being lynched. That was the first real personal sense that I got about racism in America and what it meant in terms of our vulnerability and why we had to continue to work to overcome the kinds of racist policies and behaviors that were causing us all to suffer.

That was followed by the assassination of Dr. Martin Luther King, Jr., the riots and all those kinds of things. So when you see a movie like *Selma*, historically what you see is a people taking a non-violent approach to gain their rights. You see a leader who has been jailed and ridiculed, accused of every manner of poor behavior, but who stood tall through non-violence, guiding our people towards the attainment of their rights. Therefore I think it's an incredibly important story that should be seen and discussed in a context. It's not enough to just see the movie. You have to have some conversation after the movie to understand its importance in the life of every American, and not just African Americans.

**JS: Mrs. Byrd, the movie begins with a depiction of an event that changed your life, doesn't it?**

**KB: Oh yes and that was the girls being killed in the Birmingham church bombing. I just couldn't understand how people could love God but then kill someone while they were worshipping, especially children. As I were talking the civil rights tour in 2013, I went to the church, saw where it happened and talked to the young woman who was not injured because she left the restroom. It just keeps me in mind that as a group of people, we have to keep these things before us, otherwise history will repeat itself.**

OB: I think we're pleased at the progress we've made as a people in actually being a part in every aspect of American life, but we can't afford to forget what we came through, and what we came through not that long ago.

**JS: In Israel, every person who serves in the military – and every man has to serve three years and every woman two – one of the last parts of their basic training is to go up to the top of Masada where the Jews were surrounded by the Roman in 70 Ads. Before the Romans took them, everyone in Masada had committed suicide. The military recruits are confronted with the theme from Masada, which is "never again." Israel has done a great job with their technology and agriculture in**

**maintaining the past, while at the same time moving forward. We certainly want to see the same dynamic for our African American community. Oliver, you have taught at CUBM. Talk to us about the experience of teaching.**

OB: I love teaching. What I really wish to do as a retiree would be to teach. I have had a lot of teaching experience. I have taught at Chatham College, and the class was on the economics of black community development, way back when that topic wasn't popular. I have also taught for the American Banking Association, a marketing and bankers course, for about eight years.

One of the more interesting experiences I have had teaching is at the Center for Urban Biblical Ministry, particularly because the student there isn't your traditional student. These are students who often are older, work full jobs and carry on full lives with families. And yet they are eager and thirsty to learn and continue learning. I have taught courses there such as micro and macroeconomics, as well as accounting, finance, and computer technology, and courses like that. It's been a real job to teach them, especially to teach them with the idea that we are Christians. And so the perspective that we take and the examples we use are often out of our Christian experience, as opposed to the kinds that you typically see in other institutions.

**JS: And you would be a natural for online teaching because of your love for technology.**

OB: Online education is a major part of our future. When I talk about futures and the predictions we make, most people think about John Naisbitt and his book *Megatrends* from a couple decades ago. One of the megatrends today is the availability of education to anyone and everyone who wants it. Due to technology, we can go to the Internet and learn about practically any subject we desire. The fact that you can do it remotely like that means you can have access to the greatest minds in the world while you are sitting in your dining room.

I was fortunate at Harvard to be exposed to some of the world's greatest thinkers. I didn't mention a lot of them, but people like Dr. Ephraim Isaac and people like Vernon Jordan, Jessie Jackson, were all there at one time or another sitting at the dining room table. We had a soul table, and we would talk about the issues of the day. And to be able to do that one-on-one like that in a personal and intimate kind of way was really important. Today, with online learning, you can still do some of those kinds of things and do it with a wider audience than was ever possible.

**KB: One of the things I am curious about is if you have a life defining moment or a life altering experience that you can share with us.**

OB: I think probably the single biggest life altering experience was the death of father. He was 57 years old and he died three days following my 26th birthday. That was significant because it was the first death we had experienced in our family. It truly was like altering because it meant that because family was so important to myself and my family, the loss of a member of the family was quite traumatic. Within the past 365 days, I've lost my mother, my favorite aunt, and my older brother – they have all gone on to glory. That's a good thing, but it's also really traumatic as far as life-altering experiences. Life will never be the same again, but one of the lessons we learned from that is you have to carry on. We don't know God's purpose for anyone, but we trust in Him, that whatever He has done, He has done for a reason. Sometimes it is merely that we should know that He is God and that He has something in store for each and every one of us. We need to go on and continue to do His work and His will here on Earth.

**JS: Oliver, what did your dad do?**

OB: My dad was a steel worker! He started out as a third helper at the Homestead Works of United States Steel. He worked there for 27 years.

**JS: And you had two brothers?**

OB: Two brothers. An older one and a younger one. The older one passed away in December of just last year.

**JS: And they all stayed in Pittsburgh? Or did anyone leave?**

OB: My younger brother and I are born and raised and still here. My older brother moved to Philadelphia/New Jersey, probably about 25 or 30 years ago, but he has always been in touch with us here in Pittsburgh. He had a tremendous career as a journalist as an assistant city editor with the old *Pittsburgh Press* for which he wrote about the black experience in the *Roto Magazine* here. He was also an editor with the *Philadelphia Enquirer* and also *Bloomberg News*, the company from which he retired.

**KB: And he also wrote a book about Oliver's Family called *Out of Georgia*, where he researched the family. I have several of those books still with us. That's part of him telling his story for his family.**

**JS: Talk about your mom and what role she had in your development. Obviously there were very high standards academically and spiritually in your home and family. Talk to us about your mom's role in that.**

OB: Well, like many people my age, no matter what you did Monday through Saturday, on Sunday morning you were going to church. Mom was the one who made that happen. She herself was a good Christian and attended the Baptist Temple Church for all of her adult years here in Pittsburgh. She was also one who prided herself in academics. She didn't have the chance to go to a formal college in her college-age years, but she was good in high school and great academically.

One of the things that she used to embarrass us when we did something at church called Scripture memorization. People were to memorize a portion of Scripture and recite it to the entire Sunday School. Well, sometimes when you do it so often, you tried to find something nice and simple and short to recite. Well, you can't get away with that when your mom, who is 80 or 90 years old, is standing up there reciting an entire chapter of the Bible from memory, from any one of the books from the Old and New Testament. She set a standard that was pretty high in terms of her own personal performance in academics. She made that something that we, as her children, had to focus on as well. She was the one who understood the value of education.

**JS: Where did you get your love of sports from?**

OB: My love of sports came from growing up in the age of the Pittsburgh Pirates and Roberto Clemente, and the Steel Curtain. Also I was immersed in the time when the Westinghouse Bulldogs were the champions of the city league in football and track for 20 or 30 years in a row.

**JS: Year after year, I'd read the sports page and read about the Westinghouse Bulldogs playing in the city championship game. The Westinghouse Bulldogs wouldn't just win, they'd annihilate anybody that dared venture on to the field with them. But your mom was a baseball fan too, wasn't she?**

OB: My mother loved baseball. After a while I was able to get the corporate box at the stadium, and she wanted to go all the time. Regardless of where we were seated, she would watch the game from beginning to end, and knew all the players and what their stats were and those kinds of things. She loved baseball, especially Pirates baseball.

**KB: One of the questions I am curious about is what your favorite community organization is.**

OB: That's a real tough question for me, because I

worked for so many community organizations over the years, and I so appreciate what they all do. It's hard for me to name just one. I can say that I love what is happening at Hosanna House. I love what they are doing at the Kingsley Center. I love what happens with the Spina Bifida Association. The areas I've seen people work in, in the specific diseases area with the health and human services, and in the arts with organizations like Hill Dance Academy Theater. I am impressed by the sacrifice that people make to provide those kinds of services in our community. And so it's really sort of unfair to really try to identify just one. I continue to be a big fan of the United Way and also the Carnegie Library of Pittsburgh. I think it's such an important organization in our community.

**JS: Oliver, in light of current events, Ferguson and other places, are you optimistic? Are you concerned? Are you both? How would you describe your mindset to the current environment where reconciliation and/or advancement of African American possibilities are concerned?**

OB: I think there's a real danger where we are today. It's wonderful that we continue to make incredible strides in terms of accomplishments for not just African Americans, but other under-served populations. That's good. We've already demonstrated that there is no role that an African American or others cannot play in this society, so I am pleased with that. But at the same time, the spotlight is on law enforcement, along with some of the inequities that exist in our society; income and equality, healthcare, and things of that nature.

What is incredibly important to me is the danger that exists at our knowing and not doing anything about unarmed African American shot by police. We know that the entire police departments of our country are not all bad, but we also know there are some rotten eggs. The frustrating thing is we don't seem to be doing anything about it. When we continue to see these examples and no difference in the outcomes, in that no one is indicted or prosecuted for these crimes, it is very discouraging. And I'm afraid that it is going to cause an element of our community rise up and say that they can't have this anymore. If the law enforcement agencies won't protect us, we'll protect ourselves.

Laws that have been passed, such as "I thought there was a risk of my being shot, therefore I am standing my ground" have shown to be very, very dangerous in the past already. So I am concerned about our future and how we go about trying to address race in our society. President Obama has brought it into the spotlight and made his comments regarding it, but we need to be careful and recognize that a person, even in a leadership role, cannot necessarily solve the problems of our society.

**KB: You've received a lot of awards. Do any stand out in your mind?**

OB: Interestingly, it's one that not a lot of people know about. It's a recognition that occurred by the Multi-Cultural Arts Initiative after 20 years or so of working there. It was a tribute that they offered to me and it consisted of an original jazz composition by trumpeter Sean Jones, titled *Master Builder*. I don't know if he ever put it on one of his albums, but it's an incredible piece. It characterized his view of my role in our community as a builder, not as someone who runs things, but someone who builds things and makes it possible for others to run things.

It also included a dance tribute by Dwana Smallwood. The name won't be familiar to many, but she was the former principle dancer with Alvin Ailey's American Dance Center Company. And she performed an original dance solo to Donny Hathaway's *A Song for You,* which also has a special meaning to me. That tribute is probably the most meaningful recognition that I have ever received, probably because I am a trumpet player. I do have a love for dance and I do have a love for the excellence in both Dwana Smallwood as well as Sean Jones who represent that excellence at the highest level in the area of jazz trumpet, as well as in the area of dance.

**JS: As we wrap up, is there anything you can tell us that will help our listeners understand what made you the person you are today.**

OB: I will just say a couple of things. One, it's important for anyone and everyone to get grounded with God. Otherwise you will find yourself sort of whistling in the wind, as various influences hit you, as you grow up and become real in this society. Having that as a foundation is critically important. Maintaining your integrity is also important. Finally, being willing to take measured risks in order to achieve the goals you have is also important.

# BRENDA GREGG

*Pittsburgh is blessed with many pastors who are women, and they play key roles in the community. All of them can preach, and several have been Urban Heroes in the past. This year, we are honored to have Reverend Brenda Gregg, pastor of Destiny of Faith Church, and founder of Project Destiny community outreach center, both on the North Side of Pittsburgh. We caught up with Rev. Gregg to find out what she is up to and what motivates her to stay active and on the cutting edge of community involvement. Here is what she had to say.*

**JS: Tell us about your busy life,who you are and what you do.**

BG: First of all, I am a mother of three children. I was married to a Baptist minister for 24 years, who is now deceased. Actually, I come from a line of preachers in my family. My grandfather, who is my mother's father, was a pastor in a lot of the small rural areas of Pennsylvania. My uncle, who is now deceased, was a pastor in Braddock in the church I grew up in as a little girl, and several other uncles were ministers. I met a cousin of mine recently, who in fact is one of the female preachers of the family. So I come from what I think are generations of ministers in our particular family.

And I think that certainly was in part due to the way we were brought up at home. I had very hard working parents, and in this day and age, kids are sent to church. In my day and age, we were taken to church, whether we liked it or not. And thank God that happened to me. It was just a part of everything we did. Church and ministry were where you hung out as a young person. You hung out at the church. Your friends were at the church. That was sort of my early upbringing in ministry. I also liked working with people, so being a part of healthcare seemed to be a natural fit after I got out of school. One of my first jobs was at Children's Hospital, and it's where I stayed and worked up to being a vice president there. But I always felt a ministry at Children's similar to what we did at church, and that was to serve people.

**JS: And you were at Children's a long time, weren't you?**

BG: I was at Children's for 37 years, believe it or not. I started in medical records and after two and a half years there, I understood I really wanted to be working in the areas of people rather than medical records. I had my son in 1971 and then came back to work up on the units at Children's. Then when I was looking for a full-time job, I ended up in what was then called the Ambulatory Care Center. And that was the place my career changed from just being in that area working with ambulatory patients and eventually doing a lot of the community work and putting in some of the clinics in the under-served areas as well. It just went hand-in-hand together.

**KB: I have known of you, Reverend Gregg, for a long time. You may not remember this, but years ago we had a Girl Scout troop and we used to do a Girl Scout Sunday at your church. And it was so inspirational, because the scouts got to see woman in leadership and how smoothly and how well it's done. So I always wanted to share that with you. Because that was their church of choice. We would go there and then to a Ponderosa near the church. I remember you well and a lot of the scouts went to that church. And they would always talk about the fun projects you had there for them. And I was thinking that is the way ministry should be. So what things are you doing where you're at now at Destiny?**

BG: Destiny is a new ministry, so it was planted five years ago. In fact, we are just getting ready to celebrate four years in the building we're in now. It all goes back to kids and families. We run, of course, Project Destiny, the after-school and summer camp, are run in the building where we have church services. I try to make sure that all the generations are ministered to. Certainly, kids are part of that, and then there are senior citizens. We just got through having our men and women's season, where we work together, the men and the women, putting together a beautiful program for almost a month. So they had different activities going through the church.

I would say I do similar things to what I did when I was in more of a traditional church. I don't think I changed my style or it's just that now I'm responsible for everything, including the building, and making sure the people coming there certainly motivated and ministered to. I've had the opportunity of working with other ministers because we think of our ministry as a team ministry. I'm not the only minister there, and we try to team all the leadership up, two by two, so there is always someone they can minister with who can minister to them at the same time.

**KB: Is Project Destiny something the general public can come into? Is there a process if I had a young child or teenager that I wanted to be a part of it? What's the procedure?**

BG: Absolutely, it can be self-referred. Project Destiny started about 10 years ago. In fact, it started in the basement of the church those Girl Scouts would come to. My philosophy has always been that we had a building, so let's use it. So, we began to open it up seven days a week, after school, with volunteers, so kids could come in and get a bowl of soup and some crackers and get help with tutoring.

Actually, that started because I had witnessed a killing in front of a nearby church when I first went to the North Side. I always had that vision in my mind that if kids could be safe, perhaps we could eliminate some of the violence that's going on in our city and around the world. But, yes, they can do a self referral into Project Destiny, so they can get into the after school program or the Girls with a Destiny Program, which is out of several schools on the North Side. We hold meetings at that school and at the church as well, so they can fit into any place they would like. We have an athletic program, so a lot of the kids who can't play athletics throughout the city, either because of their grades or because of their skill, can play on one of our teams. That's another place they can get signed up.

One other thing with Project Destiny is to work with CYS. As you know, many of the kids are in placement – too many kids. Our role with CYS is to try and keep kids connected with families so they are not being put into foster care or group home settings. It's a combination of that social service as well as ministry with kids. We have a camp that we work with that is actually located in Somerset. We run six weeks of summer camp after school is out. And for three of those weeks, we are actually taking kids, depending on the age, to Somerset, to be a part of what we call the ICC camp, that is also part of Project Destiny.

**KB: Wow, that's a lot. That is so much. I want to thank you, on behalf of the community.**

BG: I love Pittsburgh. I was away for about three years doing presiding elder work for the church. And I just felt the nudge of God to really bring me back to Pittsburgh. It's a special place for me as well.

**JS: I was going to ask you, though I think you alluded to the answers, but at a time in your life when some may be winding down, you're gearing up. You mentioned the tragedy you witnessed and the nudge of the Lord. Tell us what keeps you going. Why are you so motivated? Why are you, not just taking**

**on a ministry, but also taking on a building? What's behind all of this?**

BG: I think, first of all, the call. I still believe God calls, nudges and prompts you to be where He wants you to be. That certainly was my experience in ministry. Also, ministry is everything you do. Whether I was at Children's Hospital or having an opportunity to go to Third World countries to do preaching or setting up clinics, it's all service. I have always thought of myself as a servant – not so much to be served, but to serve and be able to give back to the community. I probably learned that as a kid, because that's the way my parents were.

**KB: What are your children doing now? I remember your daughter Morgan.**

BG: Morgan just left the nest and was with me up until two weeks ago. She got her first apartment on the North Side, because we live on the East. She is now in her own apartment and works at Children's Hospital as a social worker, and hopefully will finish her master's degree. The interesting thing about Alisha is she is actually working in one of the centers that I started at Children's. She applied for a position. I didn't even know she was applying for a full-time job, because she worked at Project Destiny part-time after school and between credits and classes. She is now working in their family support center, which is in the Mount Oliver area of Pittsburgh, working with families and children. Brianna graduated from Point Park, so communications is her background. She worked with me at Destiny of Faith for a while and now is working for AT&T. They're all in their own special places in this world and doing their own things. Now, I have the dog at home with me.

**JS: Tell us about your church.**

BG: The church is exciting, because when I was at my third church on the North Side, about 80% of the people who actually came to that church were actually North Siders. What I am finding with this new planted church is that, when we looked at the zip codes of this church, we probably have about twenty or more zip codes represented, even though the majority of our membership is coming from the North Side. There has been a draw from other areas, and that has kind of surprised me, because I have always thought of our church as a community church. And certainly it continues to be. But it's nice to see people coming from even as far as Aliquippa. And folks coming from out in the east, past Monroeville and Penn Hills.

It gives a nice mix in terms of community and experience with a number of the folks we have there. We still do the traditional things and minister to men and women. We have a number of individuals who need that extra support in terms of addictions they may be struggling with. We do have recovery programs that our men work with at the church, which has been very successful as well. The church has been busy. I participate in memorial services with the community in Brighton Heights. Their picnic was at our church for the past two years. It's been nice just being a part of the community and not being a church whose building is not open. We want people to feel the call and the love of God, that they can come in and get services as well as traditional preaching on Sunday morning.

**JS: Speaking of preaching, do you enjoy that, and what have you been preaching about?**

BG: I do enjoy preaching. I think that's one thing I do enjoy. Of course, with everything happening in society today, with the new laws that have gone forth, my last couple of sermons have been more about for us as a community and Christians. We have to make a choice, no matter what the culture is saying. For us, we have to choose what we believe God is saying to us, and everybody has to do that individually. Certainly we want to do that corporately and in love and in respect for all people. So that has been sort of saying, you make decisions in your own lives. Choose this day who you will serve, to look at how you serve other people as well. That's been my message the last few weeks.

**JS: There has never been a day like this day for ministry, but it's also never been a better day to serve the Lord. We're in a Babylon where we have to compete with many other voices, and it's a great challenge, but also a great opportunity to be in the marketplace of ideas.**

BG: And we have to see it as an opportunity and know that every generation has been called to tackle whatever issues among us as well.

**KB: What I would like to know is if there is anyone that you look toward as a mentor or someone who has inspired you to do what you do?**

BG: I would have to vote for a youth director as I was growing up and Sunday School was a part of what I did. Her name was Mabel Black. She just took the time, had one son of her own, and her husband was a deacon of the church I grew up in. They just had "us kids" around them at all times. She was a singer, directed the choir, taught Sunday school, took us on vacations. That was probably the person who really marked my life besides my parents and my grandparents. She lived in Homewood and attended church in Braddock for many years. Within the last four years, she passed away, and I had the opportunity to do her service and eulogy. There were many young people who came into ministry and found the Lord through her gifts of love to do outreach with kids. I would say she was a person I would really look up to.

**KB: As we take that a little further, what advice would you give**

**a young woman or young man who sees what you are doing and wants to continue in your footsteps?**

BG: That's one thing that I always worry about, especially now with this particular church, because if something happened to me, we know God has that next person in line. That's certainly been a prayer for me to make sure I am open to who God sends so that we are looking always at who I can mentor. I have a number of female ministers at the church. In fact, one of them is getting ready to graduate through CUBM. I think I just have to be open to mentoring other young ministers, whether they be male or female, and finding the time to have them be able to come and do hands-on ministry. You can't do ministry by just watching. You need to be able to put your hands on it to do some teaching, preaching, work with young people and seniors of your church. That's something I feel called to, especially at my age, to be able to put into other people some of the love of God, and some of those things I think are so important to ministry. A lot of times we come into ministry thinking it's only about Sunday morning preaching. I always say to them that Sunday's the icing on the cake. The real ministry happens Monday through Saturday, not necessarily on Sunday morning. That's sort of the philosophy about a church and how we should be doing it.

**JS: Let me ask you about women in ministry. What has your experience been like as a woman in ministry? What special challenges, if any, have you faced? What special opportunities have been presented to you being a woman in ministry?**

BG: There are always those who believe women don't have a voice in the preaching or pastoral ministry. So I have jad to deal with some of that. I have never made that a big issue, especially in trying to deal with it on a Sunday morning. I just preach the word of God and try to run the church in as excellent a manner as I can. But those challenges are certainly there. To spend your time not trying to defend it, but in trying to do excellent work in both the community and the church. I've had those same challenges as many of the women have. That makes us reach out more to the females who are coming into ministry, even now, to make sure that there's not that competitive weight of ministering between churches and women and men. It may sound simplistic to some, but doing your job and what God has called you to do, while finding people who have like minds you can walk in ministry with – because it's not a place you want to do ministry alone. That's why I appreciate the partnerships and relationships I have made throughout the community and with other pastors, and with other social service ministries as well.

**JS: I commend you for your courage and for your willingness to step out. I'm sure you could tell us stories, but they wouldn't be that edifying and they're not really that important. At the end of the day, you only have to please the Lord.**

BG: Right – please the Lord and do what He called you to do, making sure you're not in a competitive mode. Let's all do our ministry and share it with whoever God puts in our path.

**KB: Let's talk about your plans for your future and for your ministry. What are the next things you are going to focus on?**

BG: We just opened an early childcare learning center. There was an opportunity to purchase a center that was closing and we were able to write a couple grants and get the funding to purchase it so that center did not have to close. It will hold about 32 children and has about 19 there now. We are now doing some rehab on the building and the four workers who were there will continue to work for us. So the service that particular center gave to young single mothers will continue to be a beacon of light on Perrysville Avenue.

I'm glad Project Destiny and Destiny Faith will be able

to work with early childcare. My thought is, we do a lot of work with teens and preteens, but this will give us an opportunity to work with children who are very young, to pour into their lives and to get them ready for kindergarten and get them ready for school.

**JS: As you look back, what are some of the milestones and significant accomplishments that you look back that are the most rewarding and edifying to you to reflect on?**

BG: I pastored three churches and pastored them in different areas. I was in western Elizabeth, Monroeville, and the North Side, and all of those had different challenges. I am thankful that over the years, when I have done ministry, you never know if you have done all the things God has called you to do. I don't think you ever do it all. It's always nice to hear when either young people have gone into ministry or they have chosen a field where you have done something in your life to touch theirs and make a difference. Those little nuggets that come back and say to me to keep going, because those are the things that God is most pleased with. I think right now I feel like I'm a Moses. I'm looking for Joshua to come so that I may be able to take the baton and hand it over to the next one God has in line. That's sort of where I am right now in my thinking and in my prayer life – to make sure things can continue on after my time is done.

**JS: I think it's called legacy, and we're all thinking about that.**

**KB: We're at that age, right?**

BG: We are. We're all at that age. After leaving Children's, I wasn't expecting to plant a new church. At my age, planting a new church after four years and almost into our fifth year, I think I have to be realistic that I should be planning those types of things.

**KB: What I am interested in was the teenage program. We have the Brighter Pittsburgh program at CUBM where we**

**take graduating seniors and do a year of college with them and then send them to Geneva College or somewhere else and was wondering if we could do a partnership.**

BG: I would love to do a partnership. Right now, even in the city with what we are doing with CYS, we have been challenged in the next fiscal year to work with teens and their families. Certainly education is a part of that. We do Education Sunday once a year, and we give a scholarship to someone either from the church or the community. This year we're beginning to do that again, and they'll be writing essays to get ready for that. That will be in August at our church. every day school is out, we're working with a group of teachers who have all the teens and are in fact at Project Destiny in the morning. We have about 40-some who come every morning, trying to recover some of their credits. That will go until the summer is out. So, yes, I would love to do some partnership.

**KB: That's good to know. We'll get in touch and come see your office and see how we can work together. Because, as you know, our heart and our main focus is Christian collegiate education. We would be happy to work with some young people, to give them a good start and then send them to a four-year college, which of course we would follow them through.**

**JS: Do you have websites for church or the Destiny Project? How can people find out more about your work or the church or connect with or donate to your ministry?**

BG: At the church, certainly, and Project Destiny has become our administrative building, even for the church. They can always come by to 2200 California Avenue where Project Destiny is. And the church is 3737 Brighton Road, on the North Side. Both zip codes are 15212. The website for Project Destiny is www.projectderstinypgh.org. We don't have a website for the church, but we do have a Facebook page. All the things that are happening through the church side is listed on our Facebook page. If you want to make a donation, it can be made out to Project Destiny, Inc. Or it can be made out to Destiny of Faith, either one.

**JS: And also, is there a book? Have you written anything? Or is that still on your bucket list of something you would like to do?**

BG: That is on my bucket list. I have contributed to a book that a friend of mine wrote and he is from the Netherlands. He was interviewing and doing chapters of people all over the world, so I have a chapter in that book. God has put into my spirit several thoughts that I should be writing, and I know that. That's probably next on the to-do list.

**KB: Is there a favorite verse or verses you would like to share with us?**

BG: I kind of stood on Philippians 4:13, "I can do all things through Christ who strengthens me." That has been the way the Lord has given me the command to do it. He also will provide the means to do it and the strength to do it. And that's been the way I focus my ministry and things He has given us through the years. That is my favorite and foundational verse I stand on.

# ANDREW & HELEN JACKSON

*Pastor Andrew and Helen lead Webster Avenue C&MA Church in the Hill District, but are involved in many other community activities and events. Pastor Jack, as Andrew is affectionately known, and Sister Helen, make a wonderful ministry team and they are the perfect couple to lead The Marriage Works – for the Better Ministry. Urban Heroes caught up with the Jacksons in the midst of their busy schedule to talk to them about what made them such an effective Urban Heroes team.*

**KB: It has been our privilege and pleasure to work very closely with the Jacksons. We met Helen when she was a CUBM student and is a great woman of God. Then Pastor Jackson came to school as well. It's very nice to work with them. It's wonderful when you see the people of God coming together to do His work, and that perfectly describes the Jacksons. They're a super power couple.**

**JS: Amen. Of course I have known them as students, colleagues, and coworkers. They're very faithful, committed, and wonderful to work with. They're always so open and encouraging. Welcome to the Urban Heroes program, Jacksons. Congratulations!**

HJ: Thank you so much. We are very excited.

**JS: We are honored. Let's get started. Helen, tell us a little bit about yourself.**

HJ: I was born right here in Pittsburgh, in a Christian family. I would call myself a Pittsburgh girl. We lived all over the city. My early years I grew up in Homewood on Homewood Avenue. I went to Baxter Elementary School before it became CAPA, when all of the good things were happening in Homewood. Homewood Avenue was a thriving business community with theaters and all sorts of things. We went from there to the South Side. Then I went to South High School and grew up in the Arlington Heights Projects and completed my high school education there and went on to college.

AJ: It's pretty much the same story for me. I grew up in the south Oakland section of Pittsburgh, which was a mixed and diverse community. I grew up under the shadow of the Cathedral of Learning and spent most of my youth at Forbes Field playing ball. I loved sports. It was easy for my mother to find me, because all she had to do was check one of the ball fields or the swimming pool. I graduated from Schenley High School and my educational venture stopped right there. I returned to school after 32 years and came into the CUBM experience, which was a wonderful one.

**KB: Tell us what your parents and siblings were like.**

AJ: I too was raised in a Christian home, both my mother and father were old-school church leaders. There were certain restrictions and different things we just didn't do or couldn't do, but 'm really grateful for that upbringing. It seemed to me, that every time the church doors opened, my family was there. So I grew up loving God, loving the church experience. I grew up, even though I'm not much of a singer, in youth choirs and the whole church experience. I had a very good upbringing.

HJ: For me, it was similar, except that my dad was considerably older than my mother. So I really grew up with her being the disciplinarian, the educator, the mentor and all of those things. We were a very strict home with strict Christian values that we had to adhere to. We had to go to Sunday School. I was involved heavily in the music ministry of the church, along with all the things young people did when they had their own clubs and own outreach programs and evangelistic programs, I was involved with all of that growing up. We had a huge impact on the community and all our friends came. It was just a wonderful experience growing up under church leadership. It was very important to me then as it is now, and that's why I probably ended up marrying a pastor. We are in church leadership now because it's who I am; it's in my DNA. I consider leadership in the community very important and vital in the community, in our church and our homes.

**KB: Reverend Helen is named for her mother, and she also tells us the pearls of wisdom her mother shared with her. So I never met Mother Helen, but feel as though I know her very well.**

**JS: How did you two meet?**

AJ: It's funny how it happened. We were neighbors but didn't have much interaction with each other. Unfortunately, one day my brother was really sick and he eventually passed away. Reverend Helen came to my parent's home to share with us during that time. It's funny how it happened. We just started talking one day and 26 years later, we're still together. It wasn't anything where it was like a 4th of July with fireworks going off or anything like that. We grew to be friends first, and through that friendship came relationship. I'm so glad the Lord allowed the two of us to cross paths.

**JS: You have the same story, Sister Helen?**

HJ: I remember it that way. His middle brother and I were the same age, so we actually were the ones who were friends. Since he is a bit older than I, I didn't have too much interaction with him as he said, so I didn't think about talking to him. We all just really loved Barney Jackson. We rode the bus together every day and had a really nice relationship. So when he was ill, it impacted our entire community and beyond. He was the kind of young man whose teachers from Schenley and grade school came back to pay honor to him. So he was a wonderful man of God.

I guess that was really the beginning of my grief ministry. I went and just wanted to share the love of God and all of the things you do when that happens. I didn't think of that meeting or interaction as the beginning of our relationship. I just thought I was doing the work of the Lord. We were neighbors and I felt he was a tremendous community leader then, even though he didn't see himself that way. He had his own softball team back then and would take people in the community to the Hall of Fame and things like that to get them off the streets. I thought he was a wonderful young man and could see where the Lord's hand was on his life.

**JS: Pastor Jack, as we sometimes call you, did you know you had a call to the ministry? And if so, when?**

AJ: Actually, I did. I felt the call even in high school. But like Jonah, I ran and tried not to accept my call. I didn't know it was necessarily ministry work. I was always drawn to working with and helping people and doing the best I could in the community. I guess that was the beginning of my training process in the community, because I always found myself in a leadership position. They would make me the captain of the team, or things like that would happen in my life where I was always put out front. I didn't necessarily like to be put out front, but I felt it was a call on my life to do the work of the Lord, as best I could.

I have always had a heart for the disenfranchised and people didn't have a voice for themselves. So, working in our community was a wonderful thing for me and it helped to nurture me into the ministry setting. One time in particular, I can remember not feeling very well emotionally, and I could hear the voice of the Lord speaking in my heart that it was the time to do the work of the Lord from a ministry point of view. I felt my call early in life, but I didn't accept the call until probably my mid 40s or so.

**KB: Tell us a little bit about how your ministry started.**

AJ: Once I got back in the church, I worked as an associate pastor and pastor of men's ministry for several different churches. But as I said, I had a real burden in my heart for the disenfranchised so we were led to start a ministry called Abundant Mercy. It was primarily an evangelistic ministry where we took our ministry to the streets. We did our best to try and help those who weren't coming to conventional church. We took our message to them. We also did some things as far as food and clothing were concerned. We wanted to help them out as best we could and that ministry grew. We were working with some of the homeless and gave them gift cards to Giant Eagle and other supermarkets and clothing stores. So that's how that ministry was established. We really had a burden to help the homeless and those that weren't able to get to conventional churches.

**KB: I think one of the things I found very interesting was your work ethic. I know you and Helen have had a business together. I would like you to share the different things you have done in your lifetime.**

HJ: As you noticed, I just think the world of my husband. He's a quiet storm. He is quiet and I'm the talker, which most people already know! He has so much in him, and in all of these endeavors, he would wake up and tell me the Lord spoke to him to do something and I would respond that we should go. The beginning of that was we founded and started a commercial cleaning company called All-Pro Cleaning Service here in Pittsburgh, and we did that for a number of years. At one time we had up to fifteen employees. When we were in other churches even, we employed their youth departments for the summer and would allow them to clean the senior citizens' homes and their neighboring churches. We would pay them for their service – a nice wage I might add – so they would have money for school clothes.

We did that for many years and the Lord blessed us with over thirty active cleaning accounts in the city and beyond. So we did that seven days a week, still went to church, and still taught Bible study. So in terms of work ethics, as you know, I have a special place in my heart for ethics from my upbringing. You work hard, are responsible to God first, your community and home, it's just the way we are. We work very hard in everything we do and put 100% in it and more sometimes. That was our All-Pro Cleaning experience and then the Lord called my husband into ministry and pastoring. We came out of that experience and transitioned into Abundant Mercy, and now we're part of the Christian and Missionary Alliance family. We're still working as hard as we can in ministry. This year we would like to start an outreach in the community where we are planted, which is in the Hill District.

**KB: I think your church is ideally positioned to do that. The Hill is coming back, but we don't want to forget our population that is there. And I look forward to supporting you all through that. They have all sorts of great creative ideas.**

**JS: Helen, you have had quite a music ministry. Talk to us about how you first discovered that and some expressions of that of late, the gospel choir and other things you find yourself doing.**

HJ: Even going all the way back to when I was young, there was a great community choir way back then called the Pittsburgh Believers Choir, which was a community choir, with people from all over the city from different churches. Our highlight was the last show at the Stanley Theater when they brought in Patti Labelle. We were the gospel choir that was featured. We came and did that and sang with Patti Labelle and it was a tremendous experience for me. It was awesome. So from a young girl on I have always been in my church choir and community choirs.

There is a wonderful choir I was a part of, the Pittsburgh Gospel Choir, which has since changed names to The Pittsburgh Heritage Chorale, under the leadership of Dr. Herbert V.R.P. Jones. We sang all over the city of Pittsburgh. They are going to Europe this year to tour. It's an awesome experience and you grow in every facet of your life, not just musically, but spiritually too, I was the first chaplain of that choir, which was a tremendous experience. I have made some lifelong friends there. We would always pray together and seek the Lord for our needs. Dr. Jones is a hard taskmaster, vocally you had to step up. You had to audition and all those things. It's a tremendous experience.

But I do not want to leave out the Center for Urban Biblical Ministry choir. I started singing the year I graduated. I consider it a serving position. It's a place for me to serve the school I think so highly of that helped me to put a lot of things back into perspective. I always wanted to earn a college degree, which was a lifelong dream. And I am here and owe much to the Center for Urban Biblical Ministry. I love the school and love the leadership. Thank you so much for everything you have offered and afforded to me and my family.

**JS: Pastor Jack, where did you get your work ethic? Who is the role model or what experience in your life caused you to be so diligent and focused and able to accomplish so much?**

AJ: I think there were several people in my life. Obviously my father had a lot to do with it. My father was the kind of man, when he had a project to do or when he made a commitment, he stuck to it. He passed that on to me.

I had other strong men in my life. One person I recall right now was Mr. Marino who was Dan Marino's father, who was one of my football coaches and just a great man who showed me that, through hard work and diligence, many things could be accomplished. Growing up I had a grade school physical education teacher I can recall. There were so many people in my life that showed me if I put my nose to the grindstone and was honest about my work and not take advantage of people, I could succeed.

All those things they taught me, even now, sometimes I have a feeling that I'm cheating when I have a day of rest. I am so accustomed to what they call burning the candles at both ends. I understand the need for rest, and I know the need for time away from activities. On the other hand, I'm just one of those types of people who never required a lot of physical rest. The older I am getting, the more I am seeing the necessity of resting. But on the other hand, there is so much work that needs to be done, and it is my contention that we don't have a lot of time to get it done. I am trying to do my part through my little efforts to see that some social issues are addressed, whether it be through the church or in the community work. And that's just the way I am.

**KB: A young person or someone is reading this and would like to follow in your footsteps; what advice would you give?**

HJ: I certainly would lead off by saying to seek the Lord. I know that's probably not as popular nowadays, but when I was coming along, church was the hub in the community. Everyone you knew went to or belonged to a church. There's been a falling away from that and we know the Bible says in this time and day this would happen. But I still have a real sense of obligation to tell people about the gospel of Jesus Christ and His love and saving power. I would start there. Because the family structure isn't where it once was, the Bible promises that when your mother and father forsake you, the Lord will take you up. Even if your family structure isn't what you think it should be or needs to be, I know the Lord Jesus will take up your cause and put people around you to support you.

You people need to surround themselves with people they see are doing it and getting it done. If they see someone doing life, then maybe they will see and conclude they can do it as well. That's what happened with me. I worked 32 years in the criminal justice system, and a lot times people asked me how long I had been there and said they could never stay on a job that long. I think we need to be doing positive things and young people need to be close to someone who is doing it right.

I worked for a great judge, Jacob H. Williams, who had a great work ethic. He was a plumber by trade and judge all the other times. I would see him go out and put in a water line and then put his robe on and fill in the bench. I saw that done, so I knew it could be done. We as community leaders have an obligation to do the work. It's good to tell people about it, but I would tell young people to watch me do this. When we were coming along there was a slogan. I don't know if they say this anymore but people would say, "Watch my smoke." If people can see me doing something positive and watch my smoke, they can learn a lot.

They could watch me go from a young woman in the housing projects where people didn't expect me to do anything and I now sit here with a master's degree in organizational leadership. Just watch my smoke; watch me do it. God is no respecter of person and He will do for you what He did for me.

AJ: I think I would recommend that young people get an education while you are young. I waited more than 30 years before returning to school, If I had started in my early 20s, it wouldn't have been such a struggle. I returned to school because I wanted to show my children and grandchildren that it can be done. I was so blessed to be at a graduation this past weekend where my granddaughter graduated from Indiana University of Pennsylvania. It was a wonderful thing because I am the first generation of my family that has gone to college. And I wanted to be a role model to my children and grandchildren. So now I have three grandchildren in college, a son in college, and I didn't see those kinds of influences in my personal life when I was growing up. I think it's a big deal to go ahead and get your education while you're younger so you can be of benefit not just to your community, but to society as a whole.

**JS: Good advice. Reverend Jack, you mentioned some social needs that you are concerned about and would like to address. Would you care to share what those are?**

AJ: One of the things, and it's no secret, is that the family unit in the urban areas has been fractured. There are so many younger men who don't have fathers or live-in fathers. We can see the results of that in the community. Therefore, one of the things on my heart is work towards bringing the family unit back together again. I know it's a daunting task, but we have to work towards making the family function again. We have to try and do it one family at a time, which leads me to one of the ministries we have been doing called The Marriage Works. That ministry is designed to enhance marriages. It's also for engaged couples and for couples in general, whether they are cohabiting or just dating. I believe in my heart that God set it up for us to be in a family. What has happened is we have too many of these modern families around, like the television shows, and they are all dysfunctional and we seem to celebrate their dysfunction. We need to get the family unit back in order as God sees fit.

**KB: What are you doing with The Marriage Works? I know you have an event coming up.**

HJ: With The Marriage Works, we have transitioned to a little bit of a new area. It started off doing ten sessions, and because of time constraints, we looked at doing some new things. We went to five sessions and start with two sessions on communication and decision making. We then go on to cover some budgeting and finance, intimacy, and a lot of things in those five weeks. We now do a big celebration at the end, because we think it's important when you're married, that you do a lot of things together. So we think it's important to celebrate and we have a big event. Our last group was fourteen couples who participated, so we are going to take them to a celebratory event at Dave & Buster's and have a nice date night. We think date night is important. We moved our sessions to a Saturday night date night and have people come out to eat a meal and whatnot where they can let their hair down and enjoy their spouses. Even if they are dating, we encourage them to do the same thing. We talk about dating and laugh about this, and ask those who are a little bit older, what happened to dating and courting? You don't hear those words anymore. We even work with couples who have been together a long time, because things can become stale if you aren't mindful of it and don't keep your eye on it. Those are the kinds of things we talk about in The Marriage Works.

**JS: What do you think your most significant accomplishment is up to this point in your life?**

AJ: Mine is still in the works, but getting my associates degree at the age of, well I'll say 60-ish – that was one of the greatest highlights of my life. I can remember being young and hearing people make comments that I would never amount to much. At this point in my life to get my degree was a big deal. Now I'm continuing my education and my next step is my bachelor's degree, which I am working towards. Just to get the associates degree was an outstanding moment and a great accomplishment as far as I am concerned. As some know, at that time I was working the midnight shift and would work all night and try to get a little studying in before I went to sleep in the evenings. So it was a real struggle for me and by the grace of God I got through it all. And I have to say that with the fine instructors at CUBM, they really gave me some help and tools as far as managing my time and just the whole nine yards. I thought I never would have been able to make it without the instructors helping me along.

**KB: I remember Pastor Jack dropped out for a while and then he came back. That was a tribute his tenacity and determination to get a degree. I remember talking to him when he did come back and he said he was going to finish it. I have the greatest respect to you for doing that.**

HJ: I am very proud of the master's degree I earned. I'm looking forward to going on and doing some other things. But as I rethink it, I really want to tell you that by marrying Jack, God really blessed me with the best husband and help-mate. And I would not have been able to earn my degrees without him. I want to acknowledge what Karla when she referred to him dropping out because we couldn't afford for both of us to go to school at the same time. Jack dropped out so I could finish, supported me the whole way through and made sure I had lunch money and book bags. He would drive me to school and come pick me up. People didn't know that was the reason he dropped out, so I am very proud of him coming back. I think it's a great thing in my life to have him as my husband and best friend.

**JS: Pastor Jack, tell us about your church.**

AJ: The church I pastor is the Webster Avenue Christian and Missionary Alliance Church located in the heart of the Hill District. Our church does not have a large membership yet, but it's a great church. It's not great because of anything I am doing, it's great because God is great. It's been a struggle at times trying to break old and traditional thinking, but it's been a good experience. We are located within a rock's throw to three larger established Baptist churches right around every corner.

We believe, however, that we have a niche in the community we are in. They are doing some revitalization in our area and we are located close to the Bedford Dwelling Housing Projects. We are now attempting to do some evangelism in the area and have started new programs. We established a movie night once a month that has been well attended. We are just trying some new and progressive things.

Since I have been there we also started a free bread program for members in the community and we do that twice a month. We have clothing drives. We've done a shoes for Kenya drive. We're just on the move. I've been the kind of person who isn't always the most patient in the world, but the Lord is teaching me patience. We're taking it one step at a time and we are making some headway. We are trying to do technological kinds of things in the church to move ourselves into the 21st century. It's been a challenge, but it's been a good one.

**KB: I would agree. I visited the church and know you have two services now. I've seen growth since I have been there two or three times over the year. And I think people are friendly and welcoming and that has to do with the leadership.**

**JS: I have been there and have had the privilege of speaking and have been very well received. And the Jackson's commitment to education has spilled over into their congregation. I've gotten to know many of their members through our classes. They're committed and astute people of the Word, very opening to learning – committed to excellence and always do great work. Part of that is Helen's recruiting, but part of that is both Helen**

**and Andrew's personal commitment to learning, which I think has rubbed off on the people. That is so commendable and part of the discipleship process. We've been the beneficiary, not just of the Jacksons, but of the people they work with. So thank you Jacksons for enriching our lives.**

**What's yet on the agenda for you two? What's on the bucket list that you want to do, personally, ministry wise, missions, publishing? Give us the lay of the land for the future.**

HJ: I have a bucket list. One of the things I did when I was quite young was put a list of things I wanted God to give me in my Bible. There are a few that have been crossed off now educationally. I would like to go earn my Ph.D. I also started a book, but I learned some more things about that process just yesterday. Ministry wise, as my husband said, while there is just so much to do, the more you do, the more there is to be done in terms of helping the community and families. I would really like to have a great Vacation Bible School/Back-to-School event at the church before the end of the summer, along with giving away some clothing. That's really what I want to achieve this summer. That's my short list.

AJ: As far as I'm concerned, I've always looked at the local church as a hub for the community, not just the religious aspect, but to be involved in the community financially and socially. So one of my goals, and I don't know if I am being realistic or not, is that the lights of our church never go off. That we would be the kind of church that, make ourselves available to our community 24 hours a day. That being said, Mrs. Byrd mentioned that we started a 9:00 service. There were some people who were naysayers about that. But we are growing and because of the 9:00 service there are people coming who aren't members of our church, but they live in the community and come at our 9:00 service and then go to their church service. We want to continue to be available. I guess that's the right word. We want to be available to the community and be of help to the community. My goal is to have the church where our lights will never go off, where we're 24 hours a day doing ministry.

**JS: And course that is what is going on over at ACAC, your big brother church over on the North Side. It really is a blessing. The building opens at seven in the morning and the last service attendant leaves at ten or eleven at night. The question being asked today is, "If your church disappeared would your community notice? Would it be missed?" I think you both have the same attitude and philosophy towards ministry. We know you will succeed in that because if you weren't in our lives, you would be greatly missed. There would be things we could not do. And you are looking to replicate that in the church and your community and in The Marriage Works program. We know it's already happening and will happen even more as you continue to be who you are.**

URBAN HERO

# DR. HERBERT V. R. P. JONES

*Dr. Jones was the last interview for this year's Urban Heroes program. We caught up with him in New Orleans, and we were surprised that he was even available then and there. As you will see from the interview, Dr. Jones has found a niche in music and serving the Lord that is unique, and God has obviously used him to touch many lives. So please enjoy this interview with the one and only, Dr. Herbert V. R. P jones.*

**JS: Dr. Jones, welcome to Urban Heroes. You're in New Orleans as we conduct this interview, are you not? That's kind of close to your home territory, isn't it? Aren't you from Mississippi?**

HJ: I am. I'm originally from Jackson, Mississippi.

**JS: Can we ask what's going on in New Orleans? Is this business or ministry or both?**

HJ: Absolutely. This is the annual convention of the Gospel Workshop of America, of which I serve as the administrative assistant to the academic dean. This convention, if you are familiar with, has chapters worldwide and we meet annually at the end of July.

**JS: I was going to say, if you're the administrative assistant with your credentials, I'd love to see what the dean looks like. Because you're positive rap sheet would take up the whole show to read your accomplishments and degrees and the things you have done. Tell us a little more about you. Just give us some more background that will help us understand how you got to where you are today.**

HJ: I am an undergraduate of two institutions, Morehouse College in Atlanta and Jackson State University, with degrees in vocal performance and choral conducting. I also have a Master of Divinity, with concentration in drama, dance, and theology; master's in choral conducting; and my doctorate is in choral conducting, performance pedagogy, and choral music education, with a concentration and specialization in African American sacred music, spirituals, and gospel music.

Academically, I have taught at all levels – elementary, junior high, the private school sector, and with 80% of my teaching experiences being at the university levels. My specialization, as I mentioned, with the African American spirituals, is of the music of the late composer Moses George Hogan, Negro spiritualist, arranger, and composer. I am considered to be the authority on his music. As a matter of fact, my dissertation is the basis for the PBS documentary on Moses Hogan being filmed now. And they are here in New Orleans filming what I am doing this week, which is the concert in tribute to Moses Hogan and the late Glenn Edwin Hurley. The PBS team came down and not only did they film that concert and do interviews with family members in attendance and me, but they also are here with us in the academic division of Gospel Music Workshop of America.

**JS: We have music royalty here.**

**KB: Yes, we do. I've been to your concerts with the Pittsburgh Gospel Choir because we know Helen Jackson. We know her very well.**

HJ: Oh yes. She is not only my sister, but she is so precious and makes such a contribution to the Kingdom and to all of us. We continue to maintain our relationship.

**KB: Tell us about how you started at the Pittsburgh Gospel Choir.**

HJ: In 2007, the late Ralph Murray, whose grandchildren prior to then were at Franklin Regional High School in Murrysville, outside of Pittsburgh, was interested, and had been for a number of years, in forming a city-wide gospel choir. Ralph Murray is not African American. He became interested because he and his family every summer spent a month or two in Charleston, South Carolina. Charleston's symphony has a gospel choir that is part of the orchestra and they perform concerts every summer. Ralph became an advocate of gospel music. Therefore, he always wanted to have one in Pittsburgh and talked with a number of his friends and business partner, asking why there wasn't a community choir in Pittsburgh to perform with the symphony and professional jazz bands – or to perform in collaboration with high school choirs, college choirs, other church choirs, and community choirs.

Ralph contacted the director of choral activities at Franklin Regional High School, who is Chris Russ, and asked him if he knew of anyone he could talk to make this vision happen. So Chris Russ said he didn't really know anyone, but had a colleague at the School of Music at Penn State University, Dr. Anthony Leech. He contacted Dr. Leech who said he had the best person in Pittsburgh and not to let him get away, and that was Dr. Herb Jones. I didn't know any of this until later on. Chris Russ the same day called and emailed to ask if he could give my name regarding this city wide gospel choir. That same day Ralph Murray called me and we scheduled to meet at my home. He came prepared with an advisory board in place. That's how passionate this man was about starting this.

The advisory board is and was comprised of David Newell, who is the original Mr. McFeeley from Mister Rogers' Neighborhood, Thomas Douglas of the Bach Choir in Pittsburgh, Joe Negry, the international jazz guitarist – that was the founding advisory board. When we had the meeting, we talked about Ralph's idea, concept and vision, and he said they would like to have me as the director. I suggested to advertise the position so the public can't say they weren't included in this because they wanted a community choir. They did that with the understanding that if no one applied, automatically I would become the director. But if someone else applied, I would still be considered. There were three applicants, and of the three, one of them withdrew because he received another offer in California. That left two applicants and the other person never followed through with the application process.

I said to Ralph over and over that it was divinely ordered because God has a way of doing what He does, and that's be God because his desire and the board's desire was for me to be the founder and director of the Pittsburgh Gospel Choir. That's how it started and how I became the founder. I started with four people, and it was a quartet. I worked with those four and rehearsed. I worked with them on technique and concept of African American sacred music, sacred choral music, the gospels, spirituals, anthems, the history of African American influence of music of all styles and genres. We moved from four people to 25 people to 50 people. When we had the debut concert on November 15, 2008, there were 3,000 people in the audience. We performed with the River City Brass Band, and the rest is history.

**JS: God's hand was obviously in it all. Psalms 75 says promotion doesn't come from the east or the west, it comes from the Lord. Now let's go back a little bit. Where did all this musical interest come from? Was it in your family? And how did it manifest itself early on in life that led you to where you went to school and got your degrees? But go back even farther and talk about the genesis of your musical interests.**

HJ: My dad used to always say, when people talked about his child being gifted and talented and very giving as it relates to the expertise God had given me, "He has everything because his dad can't even play the radio without getting static, so it has to come from God." My voice teachers used to say I was born with the voice already in the right place, and that all I needed was the vocal coach and technician to develop and strengthen that. My interest in music has been from birth. I have always been fascinated by three main things. The Bible, where I could read biblical stories and it was my number one book. I was fascinated by the word of God, and my mom said it was because I had a calling on my life. She and my dad, along with my siblings and family members and church, were going to protective and nurture that. In elementary school, Mrs. Green was my music supervisor from first to seventh grade. I learned to read music when I was in second grade. With Mrs. Green being my music supervisor, my love for choral music started developing, because we had an elementary school choir that was exceptional, and we were featured in a number of Mississippi teacher's associations meetings and in different events on televisions, as well as some tours across the state.

When I was in high school, Mrs. Celia W. Carr, who is the reason I am in music to this day, had one of the outstanding choral programs in the state of Mississippi. Even though it was competitive between the different programs and schools, there was always a collaboration taking place among these choral directors and programs, where we not only learned from them in the classroom setting, but we learned more because we spent summer camp with them where we learned music theory and music history. They developed a camp every summer where the focus was on the music of African American composers, African American sacred choral music, and gospel music and its connection with classical music. That was referred to at that time as refined gospel music, where you bring all your Euro-centric technique to gospel music and apply it in that manner. My interest increased more and more.

There was always this feeling and spirit that came over me when I sang spirituals or studied the composers – their lives and their compositional styles. Then that love started growing and I started researching and became even more interested in that. At the same time I didn't want to compromise my Euro-centric training or academic setting, so that it became more and more legitimate in academia. My desire became so strong, I prayed to God and said, "God, if you just let me graduate from school and I will go to college and I will serve you. Let me go to graduate school and I will serve you. Let this be my ministry. I will serve you until you call me home." God has blessed me to do that. I love what I do, have always loved what I do, and will continue to love what I do. I was called, chosen, and I am humbled, grateful, and thankful. This is who I am as it relates to my ministry of music and academia. I always do bring to academia, where I am spiritually. I bring my spiritual aspects into where He has blessed me to be academically.

**JS: Good summary. I was at Bethany Baptist a couple weeks ago where I believe your title is now Minister of Music. With all you do and how busy you are, why take the time to be the music minister in a local church? Why do that? What's your reasoning and philosophy?**

HJ: First, let me give you a quick historical synopsis of how that came about. I was the music director prior to the title of Minister of Music. I became Music Director at Bethany because the music ministry of the church wanted to rebuild its entire music ministry within the church setting. They wanted someone in the position to take them higher in the Kingdom as it relates to the entire corporate worship experience, and specifically with the music. So the music ministry committee and chairperson there put in place an interim minister of music who was already on staff. He contacted me to say I was recommended for consideration for Music Director at Bethany and to formulate and grow this new church choir for the worship experiences at Bethany. The church choir is called the Sounds of Worship. Everything was revamped as it relates to that. We met and at the first meeting I talked with Dr. Gloster and shared with him that I am humbled and honored by this recommendation, and I would like for us before we started talking business, what the vision is the church and pastor have, that we would just spend the first two weeks in prayer going before the Lord for His direction and His purpose in all of this in the whole interview process. He was in agreement with that and took it back to the trustees and deacons and we all rallied to that. After the first two weeks of praying for God's direction, we talked about how I was recommended by a colleague. We met and planned in the months of October and November.

But when they told me they just couldn't afford me, I stopped him in his tracks and said I was humbled and began to weep, because I was even being considered for this position. It wasn't about the money, and I was just blessed. I know it was God's divine will that I was there because it's not about the money. This is soul-winning process. We have to become more and more imminent. I am the chief Levite in that. I am the current Jedaiah and we're going to go to the next place in the Kingdom. They went and ran with that, and the opinion of the trustees was that they wanted me to be the Minister of Music but knew they couldn't afford me. There was an understanding that it was about educating people to the seriousness of the role of the minister of music at church.

**JS: You really did it right and did it spiritually. And in spite of all the credentials and experience, put forth a great example of how to trust in the Lord and how to wait on God.**

HJ: I'm a firm believer in that and say it to my singers and choral members all the time, along with anyone I am witnessing to: waiting time in God is not wasted time.

**KB: Amen to that. Is there anyone who you have looked at and are following in their footsteps that had mentored you?**

HJ: My mentoring is a combination of both academia and being a music director. Mrs. Celia W. Carr, who is yet alive, has blessed me abundantly over the course of the past year or so. I called her and shared my gratitude to her for having mentored me during high school and told her she is the reason I am in music to this day. She said something and I just broke down and wept. She said that it was a pleasure, honor and blessing to have taught me growing up, and that I made her godly proud and followed me through my undergraduate years all the way to my doctorate. That was an even more humbling experience. The second is the late Dr. Wendell Waylan, who was the head of the music department at Morehouse College, up until the Lord called him home.

**JS: How do you stay sharp, refresh yourself, chill out, and challenge yourself to maintain the high standards you have?**

HJ: I am an active member with the American Choral Directors Association. I'm on the ministerial staff of my church, Pentecostal Temple Church of God and Christ, where I serve as a quasi-administrative assistant to our jurisdictional prelate, Bishop Lauren E. Mann. I am the jurisdictional convocational coordinator. I do a lot of reading. I walk seven miles a day. I do a lot of self-assessment to look where I am as it relates to the gifts and crafts God has entrusted to me, and how can I better strengthen them. I conduct workshops, attend conferences and seminars, to better myself as a leader.

**KB: I would be interested in learning if there are any Bible verses you have patterned your life on, for your foundation, or a particular book of the Bible.**

HJ: The book of Psalms, the book of Ecclesiastes, especially Psalm 91, which has been my mainstay. I always try to make everything I do have some kind of connection to the fact that it's here because God has willed that for my growth in some area that needs strengthened. Until we see His face we will always have something that needs strengthening and needs to be improved, or needs to be expanded. People know worldwide, and I make no apologies for saying it to them, that I am not here to be liked. But in order to see God and peace, you have to love me. So you may not like my pushing you to come out of your comfort zone, but that's part of my calling. I'm here to challenge you to see where you need to go.

I would like to see where it is that we need to be in the Kingdom. We can't settle for mediocrity. It has no place in the Kingdom. Mediocrity is top of the bottom. That's not God. I don't do stress. Stress is not of God. Why stress yourself over a situation that you have no control or that you can't change? Only God can change that. Go to Him and leave it to Him. Sometimes you have to go through the fire. He has taken me through the fire to get where I am. I have a strength that is not my own, and that takes me through. So that verse in Psalm 91, is the one that drives me. Even in the midst of all of that when the turmoil comes, I don't look at the circumstances, I look in the center of the storm, which is the peace. And that is the source that carries me through to ride the storm.

**JS: You have accomplished so much. What is still on the bucket list? What mountain remains to be climbed for you?**

HJ: To do more of the same. I'm always asking God what more He would have me do and make it clear, and help me to understand the difference if it's what I want to do or if it's what You would have me to do.

**JS: You put quite a premium on that when you describe how you came to know your role at Bethany. A basic question we get**

**a lot, especially from our students, is, "How do you know the will of God?". What pointers or advice can you give someone who is asking that same question?**

HJ: My response is if you want to know your place, then ask. Take it to the natural. If you want to know what it is that makes the elements come together to form salt, then you need to ask, research, study, and then a lightbulb goes off because there is an understanding. Now let's move that to the spiritual aspect and the biblical aspect. Sometimes we have knowledge, but we don't understand. Sometimes we understand, but we don't have the knowledge. Therefore, we need to ask God for how to bridge that. If there is a gap in our family, how can that bridge be fixed? And trust and believe him to make sure that is going to happen. It's like praying for an A on an exam and you don't crack the book to study. Well, duh! And understand that He will manifest that either directly or indirectly. Someone will be placed in your path or life to help you understand or to confirm this is where He would have you to be. But we have to go before Him and ask Him.

**JS: If God wants us to do His will, and of course He does, He must reveal to us what that will is. Our posture just has to be to receive, but the rest is up to God. Not in a passive sense, but we listen, we watch, and the next phone call, the next chance meeting we have is an answer to the plea and the cry of "God, what is it you want me to do?" And obviously looking at your resume and credentials you understand that balance of waiting and actively seeking.**

HJ: The Heritage Gospel Choral of Pittsburgh was birthed in my spirit last summer. Their very first meeting was initially by invitation only on August 13, 2014 to form this group. And how it came about was that it got to the point that the Pittsburgh Gospel Choir was seven years old, but there was a spirit of wanting to control from people not necessarily from within, but from some members of the advisory board, to the point they were saying they wanted me and the choir not to do prayer before rehearsal or after rehearsal - that it could jeopardize any funding.

So when that statement was made, when that was asked to be in place, I immediately tuned a deaf ear to everything else. I made a statement that they could not tell me that I could not pray as an individual, first of all or that I should not pray, second of all. Thirdly, you have jeopardized yourself by making that statement. Number four, that's it, in prayer from April to May, I prayed to God for direction. There is not anyone who can say we should not pray. That's going to be a problem. The choir was livid when that was mentioned.

So I resigned as founder and conductor of the Pittsburgh Gospel Choir on June 30th of that year, and the choir walked. I walked. I prayed for God's direction that if this was what He would have me to do, then give me a name. And in my spirit he kept placing Heritage Gospel Choral. So I sent my former officers and asked them to join me in prayer about these names. I gave them five names and asked them to tell me which one they thought was best after they prayed over those names. And every last one of them got back to me that the Heritage Gospel Choral stuck out in their spirit. So when the last one said that, it was my confirmation.

Therefore, August 13th of last year we began our journey, and God has taken us to the next level. We are now getting ready for our first full year. We did our debut concert on April 26th and have been performing on several programs and have been featured at several events from our inception. This year the 2016 season is already booked, and we will end the 2016 season in Paris for seven days with a collaboration with two of the Paris gospel choirs. So God is faithful. I stand on my belief of the Word and who I am in the Kingdom and who God has called me to be and those He has blessed me to have under me. That's where we all stand collectively.

**JS: Do you have aspirations to write a book?**

HJ: The Bible says out of the mouths of three witnesses, let every word be established. The first time I was told and asked the same question was by one of the members of Sweet Honey on the Rock. We were seated in the green room of the Gertrude Castillo Center for the Performing Arts at the University of Mississippi. They were featured artists and it was where I did my internship when I was working on my doctorate. And she said to me that I need to tell my story. Later on, I had another colleague who was one of the seven people on my doctoral dissertation committee, said to me that he needs to bring me there to spend a month to write my story. I was asked by other people if I have ever considered writing my story. I have to answer your question "yes," and prayerfully that will begin.

**JS: I think one of the great challenges will be what to include and what not to include. Any final words?**

HJ: I challenge anyone who would hear my interview [or read it]. I am humbled and grateful for this opportunity to witness, but you must understand that it's about our Father's business. We have to be about our Father's business, or else we have no business here.

# DELORIS LIVSEY

*The authors met Mrs. Livsey at a seminar they conducted for leaders in the Hazelwood area of Pittsburgh and immediately saw her as the quintessential Urban Hero: humble, a servant, a leader, quiet with a story that included suffering, overcoming and dignity. She was the first nominee for this year's class of Urban Heroes and after you read her story, you will know why.*

**JS: Deloris, welcome to Urban Heroes. We're glad that you could join us. Tell us a little about yourself. Go back as far as you want and tell us what you want.**

DL: Under education, I'm a graduate of David B. Oliver High School, class of February 1964. I was the last class that participated in the mid-term graduations in February of 1964. I'm also a graduate of Allegheny Community College, class of 1984, where I received an associate's degree in science. My major was child development. I graduated with honors, while raising five children, working a full-time job, being a housewife and attending classes at night.

**JS: Tell us about your husband.**

DL: Both of my husbands are deceased.

**JS: And your children are all local?**

DL: Yes, they're all in Pittsburgh. I am the proud mother of three daughters and two sons, Samuel William Mitchell, Veronica Mitchell, Patricia Lynn Marsh, Paul A. Livsey, Jr., Melissa Virginia Livsey. I also have 23 grandchildren and 12 great-grandchildren.

**JS: Wow. That makes you an urban hero right there.**

DL: Yes, it does. I have two sisters, Juanita Toliver and Linda Toliver, and a foster sister Darlene Dempster and three foster brothers, and lots of in-laws, nieces, nephews, and other family members. And I still have another foster parent who is 93 years old and lives in Wilmerding.

**KB: And you don't drive. With all of those people. How do you get around?**

DL: My daughters either pick me up or I catch a jitney.

**JS: What did you major again in community college? And what did you do with that? Where did you go to work?**

DL: I worked for the Pittsburgh Board of Education for 35 years. I retired in 2004. I worked in the pre-school for most of that time. And before I retired, I worked in the emotional social-support classroom as an assistant.

**KB: So you can really tell us stories about the Pittsburgh public school system, right? As a former teacher, we really appreciated those people who come alongside us and work with us. You live in Hazelwood. Could you describe Hazelwood to us; what it was like and what it is like now?**

DL: It was about 30 years ago when I first moved to Hazelwood. A lot of the businesses were gone and the community was falling down. Now there is a lot of redevelopment going on. We have a new Propel Hazelwood charter school. They're doing redevelopment down where the mills used to be. And we are starting to try to develop businesses on Second Avenue.

**KB: I used to go through Hazelwood all of the time and I'm pretty familiar with that part of town. You really can't ask for a better view. As you think about Hazelwood, what are you moving towards and what is your organization about?**

DL: We're moving towards more redevelopment and building a better community for the residents. Our organization is really here for the community, since we are a community-based community-development corporation. We work with other organizations in the community to try and build a better community. With our network, we want to build a large collaborative so that all of us can work together.

**KB: What's the name of your organization?**

DL: It is called the Hazelwood Initiative Incorporated.

**KB: And your role there is?**

DL: I served on the board of directors for nine years. In December I served my last term. I served as chair for six years, and they've asked me to stay on as an ex-officio and advisor. I am very happy about that. I am also chair of the governance committee.

**KB: One of the things I see is people have different definitions of community. What's your definition of community?**

DL: My definition of community includes everyone that lives in a community, regardless of race, color, gender, beliefs, or sexual preferences. Because we are all one community and we need to work together to build a better community that everyone can be proud of. For so many years, we have not had much support from outside agencies. But now, and for the future, we have a lot of support from endowments and other larger agencies.

**JS: Did you ever think at this point in your life that you'd be doing the things you are doing, as far as community activism and community involvement? Was that an objective of yours, or did it just happen?**

DL: It wasn't an objective. I did take a class in 2005 on community leadership. At the end of that class, we had to develop a health and wellness class for children ages six to nine. I organized a graduation ceremony for that class. At that time, I was not in a leadership position. But three years later I was asked to come on board with the Hazelwood Initiative, which I agreed to do, because

I said when I retired, I wanted to be able to make a difference in my community.

**JS: And you certainly are making a difference in your community. As you look back now – and as we get older we can get much more reflective because we have a lot more to be reflective on – what do you think your most significant accomplishment or accomplishments were? What do you look back at? You've done so many things and you have a large and wonderful family. What are your greatest accomplishments?**

DL: I believe my great accomplishment was finishing college and getting my associates degree. While in my emotional support classroom, I had a nephew and grandson in that class and the kids started to call me "grandma." That meant a lot to me, because we had built a really close relationship. Several weeks ago I ran into one of my students who was a teen mother when I was working at Westinghouse High School in the teen program. I took care of her daughter and happened to be at the hospital to get a checkup when the elevator door opened and she saw me and asked where she knew me from. I told her Westinghouse and she said that she knew it, because she loved my face. And she gave me the biggest hug. And that just meant so much to me. And she told me her daughter was 18, so you know, that was a long time ago. And for her to remember me, that was an accomplishment.

I also feel that I have been, and this just makes me weep, a good role model for my children. Some of my daughters have completed college. My oldest daughter will be getting her master's degree this year and is going to try and get a doctoral degree, and I am so proud of her. A couple of my grandkids have graduated high school, and that was a milestone, because they were the first to be able to graduate high school. So I believe those were some of my other significant accomplishments. And also the fact that I was instrumental in working with the Hazelwood

Initiative and the Heinz Endowment and Propel, to be able to reopen the school that I worked in for nine years, which was closed, so it could be reopened as Hazelwood Propel School. I was given the job of signing the lease agreement and the school opened in August. I feel like that was really a great accomplishment for me.

**JS: Now you've also had some bouts with sickness, haven't you?**

DL: Yes. I was diagnosed in 2009 with a rare form of cancer called ependymoma. I had to undergo surgery and I did six weeks of radiation treatment and in 2012, I was diagnosed with lung nodules and they suspected it was the same thing. So I had two surgeries that year, one in June and one in September, to remove the lung nodules. I was cancer free. Then they noticed something there again. They didn't do any more surgery, but I had to go through eight days of intensive radiation where they wrap my body where I couldn't move. And some days were an hour treatment and some were a half hour treatment. I had to be perfectly still the whole time with my hands and arms up. I just thank God for my healing, and since then I have been cancer free.

**JS: That's great. On top of all you have done you've had to battle through all that. I think I can speak for both of us in that we were blessed and impressed by meeting you last year. Your spirit and attitude are outstanding, and then when you hear all of your story, it just adds to the impression that you make. Our community and the Hazelwood community, and the Urban Heroes community are privileged to have you as a member.**

**KB: Yes, we were delighted to meet you. We said right away that you should be one of our Urban Heroes. As you think about what you have done and what you are going to do, are there authors or people in history or experiences through other people that encouraged you to do the things you have done?**

DL: Yes. I was encouraged by Reverend Tim Smith. He was the one that invited me to become a part of the Hazelwood board of directors while he was still chair.

And I watched how he carried out his duties with such dedication, so he was a great role model for me.

**JS: How about when you were growing up? Whose footsteps were you following? Who influenced you more? Mom, dad, teachers, or historical figures who really impacted you?**

DL: As far as my religious education is concerned, my foster parents were very firm believers that you raise up a child in the way they should go, and they may stray from it, but they will return. So I've made sure I taught my children about God at an early stage. And I'm so happy to say that I have seen the benefits of this in my one daughter. She holds various positions in the church. She mimes, she takes her children and nieces and nephews to church, and she is a great supporter of her mom.

**KB: So you grew up in the foster care system? Could you share a little bit about that with us?**

DL: I was born in Fairmont, West Virginia, but I was brought here at the age of three and placed in foster care. For most of my life, I thought that my mother was deceased. But I met her at age 20 and found out that I had two sisters and a brother who are deceased. I guess I spent three good years with her before she passed. Another reason why I was able to graduate high school is because, when I was in what they called the housing for foster children, didn't even know how to add one plus one. So I had to repeat that grade again. After that, I was able to excel. When I graduated from community college, I graduated with a 3.0-average and with honors. That was a great milestone for me.

**JS: When we met you last year, you were believing the Lord for a house. Any progress on that?**

DL: No progress on that, so far. But I am still believing.

**JS: Which leads us to the question as to what remains to be done for Deloris? What are your thoughts for the future? What else would you like to see happen or be involved in to help happen?**

DL: I plan on continuing to be a community leader and advocate, and I will continue with my membership in the Hazelwood Initiative. I'm also secretary for the Monongahela Marston Yacht Club. So I plan on continuing that relationship. I'm also chair of Cage Vision Cancer Support Association. And I am still very active with all of the organizations and also a member of the Hazelwood Collaborative. I do believe that God has called me into the ministry, so I believe, and my affirmation is, by the end of this year, I will have my minister's license.

**KB: That's great. I guess what I'm hearing is that something has kept you all of these years. What is that?**

DL: It was my belief in God and my faith. Believe it or not, all the adversity that I had in my life seems to push me further and seems to make me work harder. I believe that a lot of the things I have accomplished, occurred after being diagnosed with cancer.

**JS: Do you think there is a book in your future? Would you like to record these stories for your children, grandchildren and great-grandchildren to know and draw strength from?**

DL: Yes, I do believe I would like to do that. I was thinking about that this morning and that it would be a great legacy for them.

**JS: What advice would you have for people starting out who want to follow in your footsteps and become an Urban Hero and someone who is making a difference?**

DL: Do not let your past or circumstances determine your future. Be an overcomer and not a victim. Turn your lemons into lemonade. All that will take preparation, timing, faith, and favor with God and man. Those are the keys to success. My favorite scripture as I was going through the cancer was that I shall not die, but live and declare the works of the Lord, found in Psalm 118:17. My favorite song at that time was "I Speak Life," which I listened to every single day, not only because I wanted to speak life to myself, but also to all those around me and all those who were in need of that word.

**KB: You're giving me goosebumps thinking about what you have been through in your life. It is truly amazing. Can you tell us a little bit about what church you belong to and who your pastor is and what you are doing there?**

DL: Before I do that, I want to tell you another accomplishment I had. I was delivered from a 40-year smoking addiction through prayer and the anointing of the Holy Spirit. And I have been smoke free for four years without any assistance from products.

I belong to Lily Baptist Church. And my pastor is Reverend Earnest Genes III. And I serve as the minister of music, president of the missionary board, and deaconess.I've been playing the piano since I was seven years old and I was taught how to play Beethoven and Bach and all of those. When I tried to play church music, especially in the urban and black churches, I was completely lost. I was reading music, and they do not sing by music. So I had to relearn and unlearn some of the things I learned. It was quite an experience. I've been playing for about 40 years now.

**JS: And you play in your church now?**

DL: I am still minister of music at my church with my other two duties.

**JS: We met you last summer while helping to facilitate a seminar through an organization called The Pacific Institute. And you mentioned before that you're making an affirmation about something you want to achieve and have accomplished by the end of the year. Tell us a little about what that seminar was like for you, what you learned and how you still apply it in your life.**

DL: That seminar was awesome, that's all I can say. It helped to change some of my perspectives on life. It helped to change the way my thought process operated. It helped me in being a leader in the community, especially being the chair of the Hazelwood Initiative. It helped me to reprogram the way I did things. And it also helped me to begin to write affirmations of the things I wanted in my life and in my children's lives. One of my daughters was unemployed and was looking for a job. She had just relocated here from Cincinnati and that affirmation came true. She has a full-time job and has also found a second job to help take care of her family. I am still working on my affirmation that I will have a new home. I am still believing in it and believing I will have my minister's license by the end of the year. I'm believing that our Cage Vision Cancer Support Association will begin to grow and we will begin to draw in more partners and be able to help those in and out of the state.

**JS: Those are good affirmations. Talk to us about your cancer support group. What's involved with that. Do you have meetings or are you just working with people one-on-one? How did it get started?**

DL: We started in 2011. Our CEO is Karen Henderson, but we call her Kay. I was referred to her to become a member of that group by the YMCA. Kay asked me to come help organize and encourage the cancer support group, which I was very much willing to do. We started out with our small group, provided exercise classes one day and then we had a group session. For the group sessions, I was the planner, facilitator and the organizer. I employed fun activities and drew on examples from the Bible of people who had been healed. I used words of encouragement and poetry and we talked about their experiences, asking them how they felt with what was going on with them.

Karen is a breast cancer survivor herself. She had this vision, and I am very delighted to be a part of that vision.

In November we held a Women of Power workshop at the Y, and we had different people come in. We had a speaker to speak to the women about the issue of blood. We had a lady come in to do exercise, hand massages, and talk about nutrition and breast cancer awareness. And it was a success. We also had a caterer for the event.

Just recently, we had another event at Brown's Chapel Church on the North Side, and I was the guest speaker. I spoke about the life of Esther because I can really relate to her story. A lot of the things that happened in her life occurred in my life, so she is one of my biblical role models, along with Ruth and Hannah.

We did a partner program with the YWCA in Homewood this year, and we also had people in from Allen's Place, the Jewish Foundation, Bynum Communication, Incor Breast Health, and someone to talk about nutrition and other aspects of being healthy. The lady from the Jewish Foundation talked about the HPV virus, for teens. All in all, it was a successful event. We plan on going around to the senior centers and doing workshops there.

**JS: How impressive. Let me go back to your minister's license. What do you need to do to accomplish that?**

DL: I need to start going to school for ministry. I haven't started that yet. I'm thinking of going online to take a minster's course.

**JS: Let's go back, if you wouldn't mind. Talk a little more about this Hazelwood Initiative. What the objectives, goals, and what caused you to be involved in that point of your life and in that point of your community's life?**

DL: I believed strongly that I could make a difference in my community. The Hazelwood Initiative mission statement stood out to me because one part of the mission statement states that we would be a voice for the greater Hazelwood community – a shared voice and not the only voice because we wanted our members and the community to have a voice in what was going on in the community. We have done some housing developments and have a program where seniors can have their houses fixed up for free.

Then we have another program where those who are low income can have their houses done at a discounted price. That was one of our goals. The other goal, which we achieved, was to get a school in the community. We also have a group working on making Hazelwood a safe community. And we are collaborating with the Greater Hazelwood Community Collaborative to have a public safety committee where both committees will work together to make Hazelwood safer for our residents.

**JS: Who is part of this organization and how often do they meet?**

DL: Hazelwood Initiative meets the second Tuesday of every month, except for August. In December, we have our annual Christmas celebration for the community. The board of directors meets once a month, but if there is an urgent matter to be discussed, then we call a special meeting. We have a membership committee that recruits members. We have a governance committee, which is in charge of the bylaws and different policies that help keep the organization running smoothly. We also have a finance committee, which takes care of finances and looks after the finances of the community. And we also have a community contribution fund, where we distribute $200 for events to an organization in the community.

**JS: You're a grassroots organization very involved in a resident-friendly way. I see the mission statement is: "A community-based community-development corporation, is to be community driven, providing a shared, stronger voice for Greater Hazelwood by gathering community input to build a sense of hope, harmony, and promise, by supporting human, spiritual, and continuing community development." Does that sound right?**

DL: Yes, that's the one.

**JS: Are you doing it? Do you feel like you're hitting the mark?**

DL: Yes, I believe we are doing that. It took a lot of restructuring and making changes and trying to build collaborations with other people and organizations in the community, but I believe we are making progress.

**KB: Is there anything you would like to add?**

DL: What pushed me to do the things that I have done in my community and accomplish what I have, and to fight to be a cancer survivor is that I needed to set the precedent for the lives of my children by setting an example. If it was God's will, I needed to survive. I knew what I did in my life would have a great influence on their lives. I needed to show them that no matter how many children they had, how old they were, whatever obstacles got in their way, no matter what happened in their lives, they could overcome them and keep pressing towards their goals. They can turn their lemons into lemonade. I hope that is what I have done with my life, and I hope this is the example they will follow. As far as I can see, right now they are following this example.

**JS: Congratulations on a job well done. You have spoken like a true Urban Hero. We believe that the best is yet to come for you, and we hope that CUBM will be a part of that future.**

**KB: Thank you very much for being an encouragement to me.**

DL: That has been my other goal in life, to be an encourager and care for others -- to show people that God loves them no matter what.

# SEAN & LOLEDA MOMAN

*Sean and Loleda Moman have raised their two children on the North Side of Pittsburgh and both work for their church, Allegheny Center Alliance Church. That in and of itself is not spectacular. Yet they have worked their way through some serious setbacks, which they describe in this interview. When you have read this, you will understand why they are worthy of the title, "Urban Heroes."*

**JS: We have several couples in this year's Urban Heroes' class, and we even a mother/daughter team for the first time. I've known Loleda Moman and Sean for 10 or 11 years, going back to when I first started working at ACAC. Yet come to think of it, Loleda was a CUBM student when she first started back to school, wasn't she?**

**KB: Yes, she was. She was a CUBM student and has gone on to get two degrees.**

**JS: Sean, let's start with you. Are you a Pittsburgher? Where were you raised? Tell us about your background and family.**

SM: I was born and raised in Pittsburgh and have lived here all of my 43 years. My parents grew up in the Hill District. I went to a Catholic school and graduated from Brashear High School. I attended community college but walked away from that. I started working full time at Allegheny General Hospital and then went on to work for a cable company before they were bought out by Comcast. I met my wife at Allegheny General Hospital in 1993.

**JS: How long have you been married?**

SM: 18 wonderful years.

**JS: Loleda, tell us a little bit about you.**

LM: I was raised on the North Side and attended public schools. I lived in Northview Heights and attended Northview Heights Elementary School. Then I transitioned to Allegheny Middle School and from there went to Oliver High School. I planned to attend community college to become a nurse. I went there for a couple of months but decided not to continue. At the time I was working at Allegheny General, as my husband mentioned. I worked there for 11 years, up until we had our children. Then I moved on to work in a home daycare called Wee Wisdom.

When our daughter was two, I started looking for work again and started working for Allegheny Center Alliance Church. A couple of years into that I went back to school and that's when I started attending CUBM. I did that for a semester and decided to go back to community college to get the foundational classes in 2004. By the time the fall of 2007 came around, I had moved to Carlow University, pursuing an undergraduate degree for social work. I graduated from there in 2010 and made another attempt to transition to the University of Pittsburgh, where I attended for two semesters. I took a break from there and moved to Point Park in 2012 to pursue my master's in Organizational Leadership. I continued with that and recently graduated in 2014, completing their Master's of organizational leadership, while still working at ACAC.

**KB: Tell us more about how you two met and what attracted you to each other. Then take us through to the children.**

LM: I was working in dietary at the time and had been working there since 1991 as a summer intern all through high school, then continued on after I graduated. Then in 1993 I met Sean when he was first hired in food service, which was my department, although we worked in two separate areas. I noticed him from a distance and thought he was attractive, but didn't know much about him. It was funny because I would tell my girlfriends as we worked together that he was attractive, but I would never say anything to him, other than hello. That went on for a while and one of my friends said she was going to tell him I had an interest. She did that and gave him my phone number and he gave me a phone call.

SM: That's pretty much how it went. Our friends told me she was interested and I took the initiative to introduce myself to her. We had conversations and interesting ones at that. We would talk for hours on the phone, or in person, and it grew from there. From '93 to '95, we courted, and I felt a strong urge to ask her to be my wife, and in 1996 we got married. In 1998 our first son was born and he is now 17 years old. We are very proud of him. Our daughter was born in 1999.

**JS: Let me just interject, they have wonderful children, respectful and spiritual. I am sure they have their challenges as all children do. But Sean and Loleda, you've done a wonderful job, we'll talk more about that later. But back to your daughter, Sean, as you were saying.**

SM: She's 15 and plays guitar for the church on Sundays. Our son is now looking at colleges to attend and is currently working as well. Our challenges in marriage and everyday life were trying to keep a sane house. We are thankful God is in it to keep us grounded.

**JS: Now you both work for the church. Any challenges working at the same place, Loleda?**

LM: No, not really. That is the way we started off, so it's actually what we are accustomed to. I see him twice during the week, because he only works Tuesdays and Wednesdays. For me it's a difference when he's there, because he has my back. He can see things I can't and is there as a protector for me. So it's actually more comforting for me when he is there. And being that we are both on the same floor, I feel like we are doing ministry together.

**KB: Have you always been Christians?**

LM: I grew up in a Christian household. I was exposed to God's word through my great-grandmother who is now deceased. She always made sure I said the Lord's prayer when I went to her house. She instilled in me the importance of having God in my life, which was from when I was a very little kid. At home with my mother, however, we did not go to church. However, I always felt a need to go. I still remember times as a young girl that there was a school bus that came around and I always had a desire to get on that bus and go with them to church. Those were the most peaceful and happiest times when I would participate in church activities. I attended the YOU, Youth Opportunities Unlimited Program, and it was similar what we offer at ACAC, a mid-week club thing. We had devotions and they taught from the Bible. Those were pretty much my stepping stones and the things I depended on. As I became older I connected with people who were Christians, and then I started to attend church every now and then. But by the time I turned 17, I had given my life to the Lord and was saved.

**KB: I think that speaks to the importance of the organizations that reach out to the community. And I know your church does a lot of that. What is your role there?**

LM: I am the director of care connections. It's partially outreach, but more so my responsibilities are to make sure the members of the church are taken care of. And that happens by way of our deacons ministry and provision of resources to make sure that people seeking help are no longer in crisis mode. But at the same time it's all based on relationship building, so we want to open ourselves up to build those relationships that need to happen so you can go deeper with the individual or family who are in need of help. We are now located on the first floor of the church offices to make sure that is happening more effectively.

**JS: Sean, has it been challenging working for the church where you get closer to the people and leadership? No church situation is perfect. Has it been a challenge or a blessing or both? Talk to us a little bit about your experience working at a church.**

SM: My experience there was new for me. I had never been in that type of atmosphere. It has been wonderful. I have met nice people and had a chance to work alongside some of the good people at the service desk, where I currently am now. Like my wife said, on the first floor when you come in we greet you and ask what your need is, if you have one, and direct you where to go. And working on staff has been great. The real challenge is with the pastors and employees working to help keep the church running and I don't really have any problems working there or see any challenges. I help people who have challenges, but no really hardships or challenges that I see or face.

**JS: Good. Because sometimes people get disillusioned when they work in churches. They have expectations of how things and people are going to be and when it doesn't turn out, they can get disillusioned.**

**Sean, you mentioned some of the challenges of raising teenagers these days. What can you share with us? What have both of you faced and how have you been able to navigate some of the challenges of raising a family in today's world?**

SM: One of my biggest challenges is I'm in a powered wheelchair. I use it to get me around. Being that I am not able to walk, it's tough helping my son accomplish things and showing him how to do things around the house and be a responsible man. Sometimes you want to show a physical side of doing and fixing things. That has been a challenge, but I have had men come alongside me to help get that accomplished. He recently got his license, so I was able to help him achieve that. We have conversations on what a man's responsibilities are in the house and outside of the house and how to carry one's self. And he has taken on that challenge and he's listened. We've had some bumps, but as far as being a responsible person, I try to instill in him the values my father instilled in me. And with my daughter, we are also raising her to be a young lady. Teaching her things as a father, having her to be responsible. Some things she has to get from her mother and others she gets from me.

It's been wonderful. Some challenging days are getting them up to go to school. That's one of the challenges I face. Coming home and having to do their homework, they have no issue with that. Just talking and praying with them and helping to understand life itself, the best I can teach them.

LM: First, I have to say we have a really great bond with our children. They're the highlight of who we are, besides God. They give us a lot of joy and are very insightful. There's not much correction that needs to take place with them. We have a lot of family time together, which we started from the time they were young, even before they could speak. It was something we wanted to see take place. We wanted to make sure our family was well-grounded. We always carve out time once in the week, if not more, to talk about what's going on in their life with what some of their challenges are.

I would say the challenge is now getting them to really talk to us when they oftentimes want to keep to themselves. And that becomes more of a challenge for me because I know what's out in our society. So I am always trying to make sure they're open and unafraid to share, regardless of if it's positive or negative, so that we have an opportunity and ability to steer them in the direction they should be going. It's more of the challenge to just understand what is being spoken to them and what type of influences are coming their way.

Although they have an understanding of God, they're just the opposite of how we were raised. They have grown up in a household with the Lord, versus when we were growing up. So their challenges are quite different than what I experienced as a teenager. I think sometimes they become frustrated with what their life looks like compared to others who are not Christians. That's a challenging piece in encouraging and reminding them that things may not look the way they look for their friends, but at the end there is a blessing and reward if they continue the course they're supposed to keep, and reminding them that we understand they are not perfect. We encourage them to try and do their best every day.

I want to be taking them out of their room and not allowing them to sit there and isolate themselves, but to bring them into the community of the household. I do that strategically by asking them to go on trips with me to the store. Often they will see it as me just asking them to go to the store, but it's really to carve out that time to have that conversation. You have to be strategic about it, because if I was going to come out and just say "let's talk," it's not going to happen that way. I have to be creative and strategic in keeping that relationship open so they can continue to grow is the overall challenge.

**KB: You brought young people to our site who were in a program you run, and they were the best behaved group of young people I've come across in a long time. I knew it was because of you, because I knew you had your finger on the pulse of everything and everyone was doing everything the right way. It was fabulous and they can come back anytime.**

LM: Well, thank you.

**KB: One of the things I wanted to ask is what your greatest accomplishment. Let's do the couple first and then individually.**

LM: Our greatest accomplishment would be overcoming our challenge of what most people do not have to face. People know statistics, and a couple like us can become a statistic. Our greatest challenge is overcoming what you would see as a barrier with my husband being in a wheelchair. It's been tough just moving forward and navigating what that looks like. It will soon be 14 years since we had the accident, and yes, we have had a lot of challenges and sore spots. But overall, we've learned to go back to the main source, which is the Lord. And we have supportive friends who help us and are supportive in the way of listening or even speaking into some of the things we face as a challenge. The fact that we are now close to having 14 years to celebrate after the accident, I would say that has been our greatest accomplishment as a couple.

SM: I would agree with what my wife said that it's been overcoming my disability and trying to raise a family; maintaining a household without going crazy with the challenges, keeping our Lord and Savior in our life and seeking His wisdom.

**KB: And individually, what has been your greatest accomplishment?**

LM: For me I would say finishing school and especially earning a master's degree. That wasn't even on my radar and wasn't something I thought I would do. That was really great, and then finishing with a 4.0 was just amazing for me, with all the things I juggled. I know it was God who made that possible, so He gets all the glory for that. Then the fact that I was raised somewhat by a single mom and that I have been married for so long, that has been an accomplishment. The fact that God has used me to break curses and generational things that go on in the family, I'd say that is an accomplishment. Again I had little to do with that. It was God's work in that. Then what goes along with it is having children and a husband to help and not be a single mom.

So those three things are the highlights I will always reference. Of course I could have others, but material things wouldn't happen if those three things weren't in place. Continuing my walk with the Lord is the main thing. The fact that I keep Him first in my life, regardless of how discouraging things are, what things may look like, I know that I need Him and need to fully depend on Him fully for whatever comes my way. That's where my strength comes from. Those would be my highlights as an individual.

SM: As far as accomplishments, I would have liked to accomplish going back to school, but I don't see that in the future. My biggest challenge was dealing with my disability from my accident in 2001. Just getting over the devastating life change took some years. I isolated myself and getting the courage and strength to get back in society was one of my biggest challenges. I was greeted by some really nice people at ACAC and they helped me to overcome those challenges by getting out and having me involved in the church, welcoming me in working there since 2008. Out and at home, I would say that was my biggest accomplishment in just getting back out into society and being a part of it and not feeling I'm a burden on others and being equal. I thank the Lord for that. I listen to the Lord letting me know He is with me and will carry me through, and He will give me another challenging thing some time down the road. But for now just doing that - what I am now and being with my family and keeping things together at the house and working have been my biggest accomplishments.

**JS: Loleda, you mentioned some of the initiatives you have**

**going on at the church. Beyond the home, what has been your approach to your work at the church and the community and what have you tried to accomplish?**

LM: You heard me mention earlier, I didn't grow up in a Christian household. When I became a Christian, I had a longing to learn more. I didn't have many mentors. It was more of a learn-as-you-go situation. When I started going to ACAC, which was shortly after the accident. I felt the Lord speaking to me that He wanted me to reach people the way I was reached. And I was able to actually put a name to it, which was evangelism. Therefore, with anything I do, when I come into contact with people, I want them to know who Christ is, whether it's spoken or unspoken.

That is intertwined in the work I do at ACAC through the Care Connections ministry. There are initiatives that are driven purposefully that way. We have the aftercare jail and prison ministry to reach those incarcerated or being re-integrated into society. We have that support group held on Monday nights, just to make sure that people have hope and understand there is still opportunity for them to live and regain what they believe they have lost. So we have that for people to come in. They don't have to be a member or attender of the church; it's more community related.

Then we also have different programs we collaborate with, such as the Dollar Bank Energy Fund. That was something we started back in 2006 or 2007, with the understanding that those coming through our doors who had a crisis with utilities. So at that time, I took the initiative to look into the collaboration from a community perspective and how we could partner. They will give someone a grant of up to $500 per utility. But at the same time, we wanted to use that to reach those who do not know the Lord. So many times when they come through the door and we are busy just trying to make sure they are going to have lights and gas. We are also trying to find ways to talk to them about Jesus.

They don't realize it's a church since we are in a community building, but we try to make sure we hand them that booklet from John's gospel and before they leave, pray with them. That might be the only way and only church they attend for that year. It's an opportunity for them to hear about the Lord and for us to speak to someone that wouldn't come to the church otherwise.

Then we have the youth mentoring program, the Young Professionals Mentoring Program, which was developed four years ago. It was strategically setup so we could reach those who live on the North Side of Pittsburgh, but who do not come into the church walls. Over the course of the years, we have had at least 35 students participate, which I would say is significant. I'll just conclude by saying that is how I am interweaving that which is close to my heart.

**KB: I was going to ask you to give us a blurb on the youth group you work with over the summer?**

LM: The Young Professionals Mentoring Program is a seven-week program that starts right after the public schools are closed. It consists of offering the students the fundamentals as far as understanding what it takes to be successful after high school. It opens their minds up and exposes them to different colleges and careers they could potentially get into. They also learn life skills where they would be able to be independent and take care of themselves - things like cooking and money management.

This year we are adding safe driving to our classes, which is very important, because many of them are close to taking driver's tests. They will also be assigned to job sites through the program, which gives on-the-job training. They can evaluate how they feel about that field and if they would like to continue on in it. So they are doing a lot of learning and accumulate between 50 and 60 hours in the seven weeks just in working and then they also have seven field trips.

They have devotionals every week as well. And because ACAC is doing the 91 weeks with Jesus program, we will also be doing that this year for the course of the seven weeks. They will be expected to be reading and digging deeper into the Word. Prayerfully their families will want to do the same thing with them. Maybe this will be a start to something new in their study time. Then at the same time, we added a literacy piece where they will be expected to spend an hour at the library and read two books that are on their grade level.

**JS: And you actually get students to do this?**

LM: Yes, but we found there are challenges, because the city of Pittsburgh has opened up their summer program. Many students want to work and our numbers aren't as high as we expected or even prayed for. But at the beginning of this year, I was discouraged about it and didn't know if we would actually move forward. We do have at least 10 kids and I wouldn't want to discourage them and not have it move forward. We don't know what next year holds, but this year we will still have it.

**KB: What age group do you work with?**

LM: 14 and it's supposed to go up to 17, but that's not realistic, so that will be tweaked. By the time they are 16, they are moving forward with work, so we may have to change the age a little bit.

**JS: Sean, do you have a life verse or can you share any other inspirational thing you do or lives you follow or things you read? Where do you go to encourage yourself when things may get a little tough?**

SM: I usually read *The Daily Bread* and it gives me inspiration to strive in the Lord's walk. I don't have a particular verse I use or think about really. I'm doing the 91 weeks with the church, of course. That's about it.

LM: I'm also doing the 91 weeks and in addition to that I love the book of Psalms and Ecclesiastes. I love the book of Proverbs for wisdom. One thing when Sean had his accident was Philippians 4:6-8 that says I should let my mind dwell on whatever is pure and whatever is good.

**JS: What advice do you have for someone listening in who has some pretty significant challenges coming up? What do you tell someone who says people don't understand and don't know how bad it is? What do you tell them on how you can keep going and turn your life around?**

SM: I would tell them to keep God first, pray, and try to get yourself around positive people to influence and help build you up. They should try to keep all the negative stuff they hear out of their ears and out of their soul so they don't dwell on it. Just keep a positive mind on things. Like I said, first and foremost, pray and get yourself into somewhere that can uplift you. That's about it. And build each other up.

LM: Without being critical or appearing as if I am dismissing what they are really saying to me. I normally respond by asking, if they are a Christian, how hard do you think it was for Jesus to carry that cross? And I say, often we say we want to look like Christ but don't want to go through the things He did. And those are the things that shape us and mold us into His character. It's what makes us who we are supposed to be from the beginning when we were first created. I try to show empathy and sympathy in the midst of it without comparing what I have been through, because they are not us. But letting them know to always be obedient and to let them know what they are supposed to do.

There is always good fruit from being obedient. It's not always about what you want to do. It's about what you *have* to do. I think that's what people struggle with the most. They want to do what the flesh is telling them, versus what God is telling them. But if you remain on course with what God is telling you to do, there is always a story, such as today we are now able to share our story with others who may be going through trials and tribulations. It doesn't mean our life is perfect. It just means we have the proper ingredients to move forward.

**JS: It's not easy to impress Mrs. Byrd. She's not just saying all she said about your group of young people who came last summer because you are on the show. They made a lasting impact on our lives and the people they met. I know that's not just a product of what you are doing, but what both of you have done. Because your two children were in that group, and they were really stellar and exemplary. We love them and I greatly admire them and you guys for truly being Urban Heroes.**

# GEORGE & SANDRA RUSSELL

*What would our communities be like without churches, mostly small churches who function week in and week out as they believe they should. These churches are often led by selfless individuals who work in obscurity, helping people in ways that benefit families, companies and society in general. Two such selfless church leaders are Pastor George and Sandra Russell, who are connected with CUBM through their daughter, Carla Lovelace. Here is the transcript of our interview with Mr. and Mrs. Russell. (Watch at the about the halfway point when a surprise caller phoned the show.)*

**JS: Suffragan Bishop George and Minister Sandra Russell. I never heard the word suffragan before, but I'm sure Bishop George will explain that to us. These two have been married for 54 years, and for half of those years they have been pastors of a church in Washington, PA. We are delighted they are part of the Urban Heroes class of 2015. Ladies first. Minister Sandra, tell us a little bit about you. You growing up, your background, and a little of who you are.**

SR: Well, I grew up in a home with two parents, but my father was not really visible in the home. He was a good provider, but was a weekend alcoholic, which made it pretty difficult for us. My parents did not go to church, so I didn't know a lot about the Lord when I was growing up. When I was about 13, I went to church with my cousin. That's where I found the Lord and where I have been for the rest of my life. I changed churches when I was 20 and got really serious and gave my heart to the Lord. From 20 years old up until now, I have been working for the Lord.

**JS: And you're a Pittsburgher?**

SR: I have been in Pittsburgh all of my life.

**JS: And what part of town were you born in?**

SR: I was born in East Liberty and we lived on the busy street of Larimer Avenue. Then we moved to the back of Larimer Avenue, which was called Braden Way. We lived there until I was about 17 when my parents divorced and then went to live with my grandmother on the other side of East Liberty, up near where they're building the new Bakery Square off Penn Avenue. I went to Westinghouse High School and graduated in 1959. I got married in 1960 and we have been married 54 years with four children and four grandchildren.

And I do a lot in the church. I love the Lord very much, and I believe the Lord called me to be a teacher in the late 70's. That's what I have been doing; a lot of teaching through seminars and such. I love to work with seminars for married couples, inner healing, and those kinds of things. And the Lord seems to bless it when I do it.

**KB: How did you and your husband meet?**

SR: We met in high school. I guess he saw me when I was about 13 and he liked me, but I didn't like him - but he grew on me. When I was about 15 or 16, he asked me out and I went out with him and we have been together ever since.

**JS: Where did he take you on your first date?**

SR: To the show in a theater. And don't ask me what we saw, because I don't remember!

**JS: Your turn Bishop. Tell us about you.**

GR: Well, one thing I want to make sure I'm clear on is that I am known as a Suffagan Bishop. A Bishop is over a state and a Suffagan Bishop is over a district within the state. I come from a family of six boys and one girl. and the girl was the baby of the family. My brothers and I ran around together a lot. We had a lot of friends and did a lot of different things by ourselves, within the family realm. I graduated from high school in 1958. One of my dreams was that I always wanted to be a social worker.

Because of circumstances in our home, my father didn't really uphold his end. There wasn't much money in the household for everyone to go to college, so I decided that since I loved to play baseball that I would get a scholarship for playing baseball. I made the baseball team, but you had to take a physical in the city league, and it's probably the same now. And I had what was known at that time as a heart murmur, so I couldn't play baseball. That happened when I was in the ninth grade. Those last years of school, I went because I didn't want to disappoint my family.

After I graduated in 1958, I started saving some money to go to electronic school. Then once I got into school and started, they raised the tuition a little bit higher than what I had. Since I didn't have the money, I dropped out and joined the Army. I got the training for free in the Army. That was in 1960. But that was the same year we got married. It was quite a year, come to think of it. In February I joined the army and in December, I got married. So 1960 was quite year for me.

Then after I got out of the service I came back home, got a job, and went back to my former church. When I went back, they felt I met the qualifications to be a young deacon, and I was ordained a deacon there in 1969. Then the Lord led me to go to the church my wife was going to at that time, and in 1970 I became a part of that church. When I was a part of that church I got the call to the ministry. I started my ministry work there and was able to develop a couple of different ministries. One was called *Children's Hour*. I specifically went to the pastor to talk about that because I wanted to be able to teach the children about the Lord on their level so that when they grew older, they would be able to answer the questions that might come to them. It was a very fruitful time.

We watched the kids grow and develop. We had great experiences. Like once, we took them to the Children's Crippled Home in Shadyside. We took a group of them there one time. And I gave the big speech that when we got there, they needed to behave themselves and do this and that. So we got there and sat in the waiting area where the kids would come. Well, I remember this one young girl had braces on her legs, and she came in, got herself together, sat down in the chair and said, "Hi! My name is Amy." And that broke the ice. We always had a wonderful time with those children.

And we were singing songs that required the children to clap their hands. The children who came with us held the residents' hands and clapped them on their behalf. It was always quite an amazing adventure. Then the Lord blessed me with an outreach ministry and we were able to do a lot of things outside of the church, such as visitations, fund drives, food drives, clothing drives, tent meetings, street meetings, visitation to the prisons and to senior citizens homes. So it was good. It was wonderful.

**JS: Sandra, did you ever think you were going to marry a pastor?**

SR: No. I never dreamed of anything like that.

**JS: But it's made for an interesting life, hasn't it?**

SR: It certainly has.

**KB: Mrs. Russell, what is your most significant accomplishment?**

SR: Out of all the things I have done, I think the accomplishment that I really look at would be raising my children and helping them through high school and college to see what they are doing now. I think that to me that is a great accomplishment. Besides that, I enjoy teaching and enjoy watching people's lives change.

**KB: And Mr. Russell, what about you?**

GR: When I started working for the Pittsburgh Public School Board, I got a job as a field caretaker up at Schenley High School. It gave me a great opportunity to talk to young men. I could see in them some of the disgust I had when I wasn't able to play ball at that particular point in my life. It gave me a chance to talk to them. One of the greatest things was to later on in life was to hear someone as I was walking down the street call out your name. They were grown men at this particular time who wanted me to know that some of the things in those conversations had helped straighten out their lives. To me it was a continuous ongoing accomplishment and I am really pleased with that.

**JS: Brother Russell, tell us about your church. Where you are pastoring now and what is the history of the church and the denomination?**

GR: Well, the church is in Washington, PA. It has been there for 70-some years. It is a small church with a small congregation. The thing about our church is, because of where we are located, we get a lot of people who come to the Washington area to go to the rehabilitation programs out there. Then they come to our church for services and some become members and others come long enough just to be fed. We sort of serve as an oasis in the big world and we take time to minister to help people with their lives.

**JS: What is the name of the church?**

GR: The Temple of God Church. It's located at 505 East Hallam Avenue in Washington, PA. And I have been pastoring for 27 years.

SR: 1988 was when we went out there.

**JS: Mrs. Russell, what did you think when you went out there? You're a city girl and now you're out in Washington. What did you think when you went out?**

SR: Well, in 1981, I was working for Avon as a district manager. The Lord called me off of my job and said the job had served its purpose. Well, a lot of the things I did there I had never done before, like giving sales presentations, helping representatives, and teaching them how to sell the products and encouraging them. I didn't quite understand what the Lord was saying to me. I heard Him, but I didn't understand it because I knew he gave me that job even without a college education. Most of the district managers there had a college education. So it took me two years to kind of wear me down and let me know He meant what He said.

So in answer to your question, prior to us going out there, the Lord spoke to my husband and I and said He was going to send us where the people needed us. We were to love them and be kind. And so for four or five years I just kept that within me. And every time something came up, I wondered if that was where God was sending us. Then we got a second word and it said my husband was going to be preaching from Chicago to California.

I thought the Lord was going to send us where the people needed us from Chicago to California, but that wasn't what happened. We went out to that church because the pastor there was a friend of ours, and he called my husband and asked him to come preach there. When my husband went out to preach, we found out my friend had more or less left the church and the people were in pretty bad shape. We had been there for three Sundays, and my husband asked our pastor if it was okay if we went out there to help the people. We were there for three Sundays, and the third Sunday I was sitting there listening to the message and not thinking anything about the word God had given to me. What I heard was, "You are to love them and be kind." And I thought, "Oh, my God. This is not what you were talking about." That's how we got there. And since I have been there, my whole mind about it has changed. I love the church and the people. I love doing whatever it is my hands find to do. I don't mind being a pastor's wife. I have learned how. You have to learn how to do that, you don't just go in and be a pastor's wife. You have to learn, and I have.

**KB: How did that come about? You lived in Pittsburgh but the church was in Washington. How did you manage to pastor?**

GR: We learned the drive.

SR: W belonged to, Pentecostal Assemblies of the World, and this was one of the churches in the organization. Our pastor was the bishop for the whole of Pennsylvania and it was one of his churches, and that's how we knew about it and got there. We stayed in Pittsburgh and were there for 23 years and then moved to Carnegie, which put us a little closer. We went back and forth, an hour there and an hour back, for years. You'd go for an hour-long prayer meeting, drive an hour there, have the prayer meeting, and then drive back. But it was all worth it to us.

**JS: And Mr. Russell, what was your approach? What did you start preaching and teaching when you got down there? What did you see the needs of the people were, and how did you start to respond to those needs?**

GR: Well, they were broken. They were distraught and discouraged. Ironically, when I went there, it was five old women and one old man, and I used to call them my rose garden. I just began building up their hope and faith and the messages the Lord was giving me and showing my faithfulness and love for them. When they got ahold of that and found that someone was concerned about them and cared, it just encouraged them. I didn't look it as a great big thing. Yeah, we drove out there all the time, but it just didn't seem like a big thing to us. We loved the people and wanted to help them and encourage to make it through, learning to depend on the Lord for direction. I gave messages of hope and encouragement. We would watch them grow in areas, encourage them and point out to them that they had grown and it was wonderful.

**JS: Both of you, looking back, who were the greatest influences on you? You both weren't raised in church, so who along the way or even among historical figures, who impacted you to do what you are doing today and to become who you are?**

GR: It might seem strange, but the person who impacted me the most is my father. Now, he didn't really follow through with his role as a father. Some might say that, well, he impacted you in that you made up your mind *not* to be like him. It wasn't that. Yes, I was upset with him for a number of years as a young man growing up because of what he was doing. As I grew older, however, I realized that instead of judging, you need to ask the question, "why?". So I began to ask God why my father was doing certain things.

When I began to understand his plight and why he did, it inspired me to come alongside someone who was struggling so they wouldn't become like he did. I might say life destroyed him because he couldn't handle it. If someone had come beside him and helped him, maybe he would have made it. But he didn't make it. I came to realize that there were a lot of men in the same boat. So I tried to apply that principle.

Some years ago I went to a men's conference, and they were talking about absentee fathers and gave all these statistics. As I sat there, I prayed and asked the Lord, "So I hear all these statistics. But what can I do about this situation?" And the Lord very plainly told me that I must strengthen the remnant, strengthen those trying to make it so they don't become statistics. That's been my approach. When it comes to in a roundabout way, who was the one who really inspired me to where I am today and doing what I am doing, it was my father. I didn't want to see other men destroyed like he was.

And I am really happy our relationship didn't end in anger. I went to him before he died and we talked and loved on one another and just cried. And I can still to this day remember tasting his salty tears. I'm thankful we were on good terms and didn't end things on a sour note. I was determined I could do all I could so that men wouldn't fall into the trap that he fell into.

**JS: Mrs. Russell, who influenced you along the way?**

SR: I think my mom, even though she quit school in sixth grade because she had to go home and take care of her brother while my grandmother worked. I think she influenced me because she was a go-getter. Even though she only went through the sixth grade, there was nothing that she feared doing., especially after she gave her life to the Lord. God would give her things to do, and she would just go ahead and do it. She followed the pattern the Lord gave her. She inspired me a lot, because when I was 10 years old, she decided to go to beautician school. She went and finished and got her license, and that was a big deal.

**KB: You were lucky and blessed to have a mother that could do hair. Back then it was a whole different thing.**

SR: It was a blessing. The only thing when she passed on early on was that I didn't have anyone to do my hair. But she did teach my sister and I how to do hair so we could do our own.

**KB: What are your plans for the future? We'll start with Mrs. Russell.**

SR: Well, it's funny you would ask that. Just recently, our

guest bedroom is used as our prayer room, I was in there one morning last week and was praying, and the Lord gave me a wonderful word and told me the different things He was going to use me for in my old age. I had to laugh and I said that I don't consider myself as old. The Lord just spelled it out that in my old age I would be doing this and that. I had to laugh at that, in my old age, see myself doing…

GR: She has a wonderful ministry called Heart to Heart Connecting.

SR: Thanks, I couldn't get it out. We are planning married couples' seminars starting Friday nights and half of the days on Saturday. These are things I enjoy doing. I also have a ministry called Pathfinders, which is a ministry that ministers to people who have inner healing needs for emotions. Once a month with our church, we have a Pathfinders Saturday. We're helping people who are having problems with guilt, depression, anger, and all kinds of hurt issues from emotional problems. I enjoy doing that.

**KB: One of the reasons I know the Russells is because I taught their daughter. She was in my first class. I remember Mrs. Russell as an elegant woman when she came to the school. She was no nonsense. And the thing that impressed me was the fact they took piano lessons. I remember the youngest boy took it for five or ten minutes. I figured, oh, music must be important to them. So because of them, Kathryn took violin. I remembered that and the way the children always looked nice in school. They were very well behaved. And I remembered you coming up and how happy I was to see you. So we have someone on the line who wants to join in, John?**

**JS: Oh yes. Carla Lovelace, welcome.**

CL: Hello everyone.

**JS: Carla, tell us about growing up in the Russell household. We've been talking about ministry and commuting down to**

**Washington, PA,, church life, and being a pastor's wife. What are your recollections in ministry as a preacher's kid?**

CL: I think my brothers and sisters would all say the same thing: ministry, home and everything else went hand in hand. Even before my parents became pastors, they guided us, taught us, protected us from things, and inspired us. They inspired us and today they're our biggest cheerleaders, regardless of what we are doing. They didn't show us church or talk about it, they took us. They didn't just leave us there to go for ourselves, they were they, so when we came home and if we had questions, they were there for us. We experienced that together as a family and still do to this day.

**KB: Tell us about your brothers and sisters.**

CL: I have a brother who is a professor at Berkeley in Boston. I have a sister that is the liaison for the inner city kids going to suburban schools at Wellesley. Then I have a younger brother here in Pittsburgh who just got a new job with Eaton Corporation. He also works at a church in the city and supports my father whenever he is needed.

**KB: What's the birth order?**

CL: I am the oldest, and then my brother George, my sister Cynthia, and my younger brother Michael.

**KB: Now who's like your mother?**

CL: Well, let it be told they tell me I have the cookie-cutter part of it.

**KB: Mrs. Russell, she's your child.**

SR: Yes, she's my child, but they're all my children. They each have a little bit of me in them, just like they have a little bit of their dad in them. The funny story is that every time my youngest daughter comes home from Boston and goes back to Boston, her brother, who is also is in Boston, will always say how he knows she has been with her mother because she is saying the same things I say. But Carla is really feisty like I am.

**JS: I don't think I realized you were the oldest, Carla. That explains a lot of how you organize things at CUBM. But Carla, did you ever resent the amount of time pastors and spouses have to put into ministry. Was that ever an issue for you or did you just join in and minister along with them?**

CL: I am very glad we were probably in college when they really became pastors, because we didn't have that opportunity to say those things. None of us were on our own, but we were pretty much where we could take care of ourselves when they went into ministry. We didn't have to worry about my dad having to go somewhere else when my brothers had a baseball game or anything like that, because they were always there. They still find a way to be at almost everything we do. So I really didn't have a reason to resent the church or anything like that. As we get older, we all have our roles in their church, even though we don't all go to their church. We all play a role. And then when we come home, we know what were supposed to do. I have two pastors.

**JS: You're blessed and highly favored.**

CL: Two people to answer to.

**JS: Carla, talk to us about your brother coming to Pittsburgh. We've been talking about him coming in April. Are you looking forward to that?**

CL: Yes, I am, because George has been gone so long. When he left here, George had music under his belt, but now he really has music under his belt. When George left here, he was at a place where, oh yeah, that's George. Now when he comes back, it is like, "Wow. That's George." Music is always something he has wanted to do. To George it's never been a big deal. It's something he likes to do and he just does it. But to actually see him and for people to actually see the accomplishments and the places he has been because of his music, it will be a big difference for people that know him as Georgie. I think when he comes he will be known as George. That's not the Georgie people remember.

**JS: Mr. Russell, keeping on George, your son. Did you think he would be this immersed and involved in music? Did you see that coming?**

GR: No, not really. Because at one time his dream was to be a baseball player. Then he started playing, going back to the lessons, and took a liking to it. But did I have a dream it would be to this point? No. I was with him recently where we had a grandfather's weekend retreat. That weekend they had a jazz conference, sponsored by Berkeley College, and George was highly involved with that. Just to see him walking around and doing what he did and the respect he was getting from both his peers and the students there. You just sit there in awe and say, "Gee, this is my son." Did I ever think it would get to this point? No. And George is the type of person who just does what he does. He doesn't say, "I am Mr. So-and-so. I'm just George and this is what I do." He will readily admit that he enjoys what he does and gets paid for it. He's a down-to-earth guy, he loves what he is doing, appreciates music, and appreciates helping other people.

**JS: Mrs. Russell, did he get his music from you?**

SR: Nope, sorry! He probably got it from his grandfather. His father's father played violin growing up, and my husband's older brother played bass. They were the musical family. My family wasn't. When George was about 12 or 13 years old, he did think he wanted to be a ball player. But when he got about that age, he started taking music a little bit more seriously. Then he went to CAPA. Mrs. Ellie Sax, who was a teacher there at CAPA, and her son and George were friends. George went over to her house one day and was playing the piano, and she said he needed to go to CAPA. He was the first graduate who did a senior recital. And as George does, he incorporated all the different art forms in the school and made sure every art form was recognized in his concert. But one song he wrote, and he was writing songs for many years, but one he wrote was *Music is My Life*, and that has followed him through all of his life. That's the way he looks at life - the music is his life.

**JS: Mr. Russell, let's get back into our Urban Heroes questions. What is on your bucket list and what haven't you done in ministry or life that, Lord willing, you would still like to see accomplished?**

GR: I want to just continue what I am doing. Every now and then I say I am getting too old and I am ready to retire and let someone else do it. But it just seems like the Lord puts something else on my plate that inspires me to keep on going. I just want to see lives being changed, regardless of who they are. I enjoy seeing lives being changed. The impact of my father really stayed with me, because I understood there are so many people that are gifted to do things. But because they hit a stump or a dream has been shattered, they kind of just give up on life. And unless someone comes along and encourages them that they can still do it and that it isn't the end of the dream and there is more to it, they'll fail. And I don't want to see people fail.

I have talked with young men who have dealt drugs and talked with them about salvation. One of the things we did at our church was the Chat and Chew Ministry. Chat and Chew was a ministry dedicated to men. And we called it Chat and Chew because we chewed on light refreshments and chatted on situations and problems that men were having, watching grown men being able to reflect on their past and sit in the group with other men and cry because they realized what they were hurting from and what they had missed. And to see things like that, that's my future, to see men's and people's lives changing, and to be able to say we were a part of it.

I always say I wanted to be a social worker. I never went to college to be a social worker, but God let me be a social worker for Him, and this is what I do. And I enjoy it. It's just a marvelous thing. My future? What do I look forward to doing? I look forward to continuing to do what I do right now because I love it.

**KB: Do you have a favorite Bible verse, quote, or passage you can share with us?**

GR: My favorite Bible verse is Psalms 71. And it says, "In thee oh Lord, do I put my trust. Let me never be put to confusion."

**KB: Mrs. Russell?**

SR: I guess the one I will give you is Isaiah 40:8 which says that, "The grass withereth, and the flower fadeth, but the word of our God shall stand forever."

**JS: You both have an exemplary marriage, being together for 54 years, in ministry and with the same church for 25 years. What do you say to someone listening about either – marriage or ministry – what advice do you give them? Share some wisdom of things that come to your mind for someone listening that would encourage them to the longevity and track record you have in marriage and ministry.**

SR: In marriage, if I was to talk to people about it, I would say that marriage is a relationship and a process and not something you build overnight. I'd also let them know there are two things they need. One is love and the other is respect. The Bible tells us in Ephesians 5:33 that the man, the husband, is to love his wife unconditionally. And that the wife is to respect her husband. And that's God's way of doing it. And when you follow that plan you can't go wrong.

GR: I'll talk about the ministry side of it. I would

encourage anyone who wants to go into ministry to make sure that's where you want to go, that you want to be in ministry. If you want to be successful in it, you've got to really love God. Because if you love God, you'll love His people. Sometimes dealing with God's people is hard and difficult. Some of those you do the most for will turn around and hurt you. But then when you understand your love for God goes beyond that and think of what Jesus did for us, it brings about a difference. So you have to love God. And if you love God you'll be able to serve God's people.

I always tell the saints when I talk to them that they don't belong to me and are God's kid. When they come in to be counseled, the first thing we always have is prayer. I need to do that because they don't belong to me, they belong to God. And I want to make sure I tell them what He wants them to know. And sometimes it hurts and sometimes they disappoint you and then you watch them grow and they begin to understand what you are teaching and they start living it. They come back excited because they have the victory over something and will tell you in so many words that it works. That's gratifying. It's not a million dollars, but you can't pay for that.

We have seen them come as drug addicts and are now faithfully in the church and afraid to go back to their old lifestyle. One individual got jammed up not too long ago and said he got to thinking about if he went back, he would have to go through all he went through to get to the point he was at, and he didn't want to go through that again. So he was just going to hang in there until God changes things. God did and he was so excited about that. You can't buy that. So what would I want to be doing? What I'm doing right now. Helping people.

**JS: We talked marriage and ministry. What about those married *and* in ministry. Carla said they were a little older**

**when you went into ministry so they didn't have some of those time and attention pressures. Still, in ministry it can be intense and pressure packed. What advice would either of you have for a couple in ministry trying to maintain and develop a vibrant relationship with one another?**

GR: The important thing there is that God knows I am married, and God is not going to put demands on me that are going to affect the marriage. To Him, the marriage is honorable. It's something He has brought into play. I think something you have to do is where the Scripture says about you becoming one. You really have to start thinking as one. Sometimes you hear people say that marriage is 50/50. No, marriage is not 50/50. Marriage is whatever it's going to take for both parties to keep it the way you want it to go. Sometimes the husband has to give 100% and sometimes the wife has to give 100%. Sometimes the husband has to give 50% and sometimes the wife does. You never know what you have to contribute. The goal is you want to see the marriage work. You want to have a marriage, not just coexist. There are a lot of people married today that are just existing and not enjoying the marriage. But when you really want the marriage to work, you're willing to sacrifice what you have to sacrifice to make it work. and both do the same thing. The ultimate goal is that the marriage can be a success to please God. And understand that anything God has ordained, such as a marriage, is going to be under attack from the adversary. So you have to bind together to keep your marriage together.

SR: I would say communication is part of the key. You have to realize men and women are different. My husband doesn't think like I do and I don't think like he does. So a lot of times, husbands and wives want each other to think the way they think. So you have to learn how to adjust to each other. I have to learn how to adjust to the way he thinks and does things. And he has to learn to adjust to the way I think and do things. So I think communication is really the key.

GR: And keeping Jesus the center of it.

**KB: That is very true. What parenting advice would you have for anyone starting off with children. Your children always went to the public school system, which really says a lot about the type of education they got way back then.**

SR: I think you have to keep on top of everything. Children are going to be children. but as my husband said, you have to teach them. You teach them at home before they go out. To give an example, I would take the kids to the store. Before we would go in the store, I would have a teaching moment of what to do and what not to do. And I told them, if they show out on me in the store, I would have to show out on them in the store. I think parents miss a lot of teaching moments with their children.

And quality time is really important. I think it's important, as my husband said before, to help the children understand that we really love them. We did not put all of our children together in a basket and say they would all come out the same way. We try to recognize within each one of them what it was God has put into them for them to do. And that is what we tried to cultivate. And that's the way we tried to push them to go that way.

Carla has been an organizer since she was a little girl. She would get up in the morning and she'd come out of the bathroom and her hair would be combed and she'd be dressed, would go back to her room and everything would be picked up and made up. I knew she was an organizer. On the other side was her sister, who was not organized and everything was different. You have to learn your children and learn who God made them. You can't make them be something they're not. And if you follow them, they will let you know who they are. You just have to follow them. And just kind of nudge them to where you know God wants them to go. And I find with children, people are not training their children these days. They aren't watching them or seeing who they are. Many parents want their children to be who they wanted to be when they were little. And it doesn't work that way.

GR: One of the things we always taught our kids and recognized was that they were no different as anyone else's children. They could be just as bad or just as good as anyone else's children. The one thing we established from the very beginning was bridges. Our kids always knew they could come back across the bridge. No matter what you did in life, because you have no guarantees in life how they will turn out, they knew they could always come back across the bridge.

One of the things I would teach the kids was they would be upset about something and I would tell them the important thing was for them to do what was right. Now if you go to Carla, you go and do what's right, she'd get a big kick out of it. And even though they might not have been treated fairly in that situation, you instill that value in them that you do what's right. And that's the one thing we did. And I believe that's what has enabled us to have the relationship we have with our kids today.

We went through ballets, piano recitals, baseball games, plays, and whatever they were involved in, we were involved in it with them. And we always let them know we'd help to guide them in their choices and decisions. But the choice we ultimately let them know was theirs, and we would support their choice. And I don't think, I know the Lord has blessed them as a result of that. I see how they are with one another today and how they still are with us. I guess the only reason they don't have a key to this apartment is because we could only get two. But they had keys to the house. You can't start when they are 15 or 16. You start when they come into the world. How many times did they bring home a picture, all excited, and want you to tell them about the picture? I couldn't figure out what they were, but then I got smart and had them sit down and explain it to me. Then they could tell me what it was. But we were involved in their lives. And you've got to get involved.

SR: And you have to tell them truth too. Whether they like it or don't. Even to your own hurt and that of your children. And if you do something wrong, you need to apologize to them.

GR: It's good to say you are sorry and messed up and shouldn't have done something. And we had no problem saying we were sorry and made a mistake. And that goes a long way.

**JS: Yeah, it does. What do you do in your free time? Do you have any hobbies? What do you do to refresh individually?**

GR: We'll go see a Pirates' baseball game. We haven't done it as much as we used to. But we used to have a slum day. And slum day was a day you got up, had breakfast when you were ready to, you might go to a movie, or we might go shopping, and just be together and do what you want to do. No great big hobbies.

SR: The thing I really enjoy doing is reading my Bible, praying, and hearing from the Lord. Now that may sound funny, but I really enjoy that. And I have learned just recently about something called "soaking" where you play some good soft Christian music and just sit and reflect on the music and reflect on the Lord. So I get rest and peace from that. Which allows me to be able to do the other things I am able to do.

**KB: Do you have any community organizations you belong to or support?**

SR: We belong to the ministerial alliance out in Washington. The one thing I've enjoyed in my life since 1995 is something called Theo-Therapy, which is an inner healing group. I've worked with them and have gone into the Greensburg jail they are getting ready to close up. But we've gone in there and we've worked with the inmates. We do weekends there from time to time and people come in for help and those are the types of things I enjoy doing.

GR: I don't have anything particular at this time. I just take it easy. I read my newspaper. The grandkids were asking recently what I do, and they replied that I read my newspaper.

**JS: Who does most of the preaching?**

GR: Mrs. Russell preaches some and does a lot of teaching. I do most of the preaching right now and we have a couple other ministers who fill in. She does a lot of the teaching and the Theo-Therapy is her baby and she does a tremendous job with that. Sometimes she brings in different speakers to deal with different subjects. But I do most of the preaching, yes.

**JS: What have you been preaching on lately?**

GR: A couple weeks ago, I preached a message and the title was *Peace in a World of Chaos*. It dealt with the chaos in the world, but how God can give you peace in the midst of this chaos. I have been finding out that recently I have been preaching messages that go to the individual. That you really have to start examining yourself and where you're at in the world. You hear a lot of different talk about the end times. I'm not a studier of the end times, but I believe a time is going to come when this is all going to end. But I sense in my spirit that it's getting closer. But my big urgency now is the saints to try and get them ready for the coming of the Lord.

**JS: Mrs. Russell, can he preach?**

SR: Yes. He's a very good preacher.

**KB: Is there anything the two of you would like to add?**

GR: I myself can't think of anything I'd like to add. Again, I just thank you for this invitation or honor. It's something we never dreamed of. We just did what we thought was the right thing to do, giving a guy a glass of water. But our kids saw something we didn't. They told us some time ago that we just don't know what we have and don't know what's in us. And I say we just do what we feel we're supposed to do. But we've never looked at it as looking for something in return. It was just something, an attitude and spirit the Lord has blessed us with, and we just do.

**JS: Well the issue of leadership is when we do what God wants us to do, we never know what we prevented. That's how we lead in faith, minister in faith, and the life that we touched was changed. It takes someone in a different direction and we never know what might have been. So we just trust the Lord for the results. You fit the perfect mold of what we want the Urban Heroes program to mean: people who serve day in and day out and don't always get recognition for that. They do it with distinction and excellence and don't make any headlines for all the right reasons.**

**Where would we be without you? Where would our communities and individuals be without faithful and committed spiritual folks like you? We thank you for giving us Carla at CUBM. Thank you for our community and your selfless service day in and day out. We can understand why God would want to honor some folks like you. Thank you for consenting to be a part of the program, but you certainly fit all the descriptions and meet all the requirements.**

# JOY SATO

*It is ironic that Joy helped us celebrate the last Urban Heroes' program as our event coordinator and this year she is an Urban Hero. We hope she gets the night off, because the program will be held at the Pittsburgh Center for the Arts where Joy serves as the special event coordinator. Joy has quite a story to tell of her time in Los Angeles, where she rubbed elbows with the rich and famous. Here is Pittsburgh, she rubs elbows with her family and friends, and you will see how important they all are to her as you read through this interview.*

**JS: Tell us a little bit about you.**

JoyS: I was born and raised in Pittsburgh in the Hill District. I had my first job at nine years old at a record shop. I always loved music and wanted to work in that arena, but my dad said no. I still went and worked in the community to make a quarter so I would have quarters to share with high school students when we would have the Monday movie. I would give quarters to kids who couldn't go so we could all go and see the movie. I stayed here until I was 18 when I moved to Southern California and ended up having a full life of 37 years there. When my daughter moved back to Pittsburgh and had my grandchildren, I did not want them to grow up without me. I came back to be with them and I am thankful I did.

I currently am the director of special events at the Pittsburgh Center for the Arts. All the training I had in behavioral sciences and health services at UCLA, I've been able to use it in working with people in every way. I have dedicated my life to other people, and I consider myself a servant and professional facilitator. When I came back here, I thought I was going to give back all I had learned, because I had done quite a bit out in California. I worked at Motown for ten years in the music industry and I am still tied to it after 37 years of living out there. I was involved in many firsts for women. I was involved in City Council. I worked in the city of Los Angeles and had quite a hand in Tom Bradley's administration with Maxine Waters. I knew all of them when they came along and I brought the entertainment industry into the political arena. I was close with Stevie Wonder. I did the first Street Scene there that brought many entertainers into the city in September of every year. I produced the first secular/spiritual concert at the Great Western Forum, with Jack Kent Cook. He said if I pulled it off, he would pay the $100,000 insurance policy, because several people had tried it but no one made it, but we did. We did that because of my faith.

I did a birthday tribute to Stevie Wonder. We had it downtown in that brand new area they built in the heart of downtown. I still have many of those ties and friends. It was where I really started, this whole thing of working with people, lifting up people's lives. My inspiration was my grandmother. Whenever I would come home, she and I would stay up all night just talking about the Lord. From the time I was seven, she couldn't read and write, and I would read to her. I still have her Scofield Bible. When the binder wore out, she sewed it up with a needle and thread. In the back of it she had a piece of paper with certain scriptures. My favorite note she had was: "What is a unique faith?" And it stayed with me so that I could understand, I wanted to know about faith and do it for myself. Today, praise God, I know it in a deep, wonderful and impactful glorified way. Our faith that is motivated and generated by the Word, is my calling card.

**KB: Joy has a rich background in the arts. And she has passed that along, not only to her daughter, but to her grandchildren. Joy, why don't you tell us what they are doing now?**

JoyS: When I made up my mind to come after my daughter was pregnant, I didn't want to have that long distance thing; I have to be there with them for them to get my influence so I can take them to things. Because I want them to be exposed to the arts, different cultures, different people, different food, and different things. More than that, I wanted them to know God for themselves. I would come home from work every day and bring mini tambourines and different things for them so we would have a program. We would celebrate their mom or dad's birthday and Mother's Day and all of that. They have grown up with this. I worked in institutional advancement at the University of Pittsburgh and then I came over to the Center. The art and entertainment piece has been with me all the way. I've brought Ozeola McCarthy to the University. I brought Martha and the Vandelas here to the Center, because I have known Martha as my friend. That was another great time and my kids have seen all of this. When it was time for Sarah, who is the oldest, to go to school, she didn't know what she wanted to do. We were going through Schenley Park at the Race for the Cure and listening to Martha Munizzi singing, "I know the plans I have for you."

Sarah told me she knew God has a plan for her, but she didn't know what it is. I told her to keep asking and believing that He is and does have that plan. Then her dad took her to a workshop in DC featuring to the director of the World Bank. The director talked about Third World countries and that people needed to know something about the economics of those country. Sarah came home and said she knew what she needed to do – go to American University to take economics and do something with anthropology in other countries.

Praise God, today she has a degree in economics, and her minor is in social anthropology. Then when she graduated, we were spending time and I told her that she would do something different than her other four roommates. She started crying and said she knew her family had given her everything, but she wanted to go to Hillsong in Australia to play her drums and do whatever God was calling her to do there. I immediately said, "Well, that's what you are going to do." She didn't think her father would let her do that, but she's there, and has been there for three years. What has happened to her is just outstanding. It's just wonderful and I am so thankful for it, because I got to see how God provided.

When you don't know the way and trust Him, He has a provision network that expands and multiplies. He has a way of doing that and leading us and guiding when we ask and trust Him. My grandson James would come to the Center for an Irish step dancing class, and the woman who was the instructor had three sons. One had already been to Dublin and won the championship for male Irish step dancers. She said she would like to take James to the Irish Center. So we went without knowing anything about Irish step dancing.

He was about four or five years old when he started dancing. James went on to middle school and CAPA, Pittsburgh Ballet Theater, which is the international network for professional dance in Pittsburgh. The ballet master who is there now saw him and called and said he was the most talented kids he had seen in a long time. Today James is signed for the fifth year, signed his five-year contract at Cincinnati Ballet where he is a classical ballet dancer and recently promoted to soloist. He is absolutely stunning and dedicated.

Him moving into that field was a lot different from where Sarah is. There are people from all over the world, because Hillsong is working in 12 countries. There are doctors, lawyers and people with professional positions who have stopped what they are doing in their trained categories to go there and study the leadership program that Brian Houston has developed. But James, during the summer months, has had different choreographers call him. His summer is so packed that he will be at the famous Joyce Theater, where most people get started, for the second time. We are just so proud of both of them. The first thing we do when we take them anywhere is to get connected to a church. And they have both maintained that. For me to go to DC when Sarah was going to school and standing there with her with her hands up in the air, I'm crying great tears of joy. It's the same thing with James. He comes in and I hear him thanking the Lord for not having any injuries, for all He has done for him. How can I not be grateful and so thankful for what He has done for me?

**JS: You spent some time in North Carolina when it wasn't the easiest time for people of color to live in the South. Yet, you've gone on to impact the world. You alluded to your grandmother. Talk to us about your experience in the South, what it gave you, what it did for you, and what was your impetus to not allow that to shape your life, but to go on to one of the centers of the world for entertainment and make your mark?**

JoyS: I believe it had more of an impact on me than I thought it did at the time. I say that because I did not go to high school here in Pittsburgh. I wanted to go and live with my mother in North Carolina. So my father agreed to let me go there and stay with her. I went to a little school and graduated with only 49 people. It was a time when black children had to stay home to help farm the land, as opposed to coming to get an education. Any of us who got through, it was exceptional feat.

The most impactful teacher was Simona Lee. When you came in, she would call you by your last name, and she had no tolerance for foolishness. The impact she had on all of us was profound and left such an impression on us. I was in the choir and won lots of awards with our school. I was a champion basketball player before women's basketball ever came along; the trophy is still there in North Carolina. My mother knew how to sew and she could make anything. So she would make me beautiful skirts and blouses out of chicken feed sacks.

Whenever we would go out into the community, we were going there to apply for jobs. I had won a typing contest for the entire county, and I could type 100 words a minute. I would walk in and say I would take any test they would give me. And the reason they would not hire me was not my skills, it was because I was African American. People would call my mother up and tell her I was coming in the front door, because I was defiant. I wanted someone to tell me why they wanted me to use the back door.

But as we grew and I graduated and went on to California, it was a whole different lifestyle with different people and different cultures. I had so many different kinds of friends on the West Coast. I met my husband, David, at UCLA. I got completely away from the South as an African American, it's not that you forget, for you remember what has happened to you. But I never wanted that to define who I am. And I have done that with my children as well. You accept people for whoever they are because God made all of us. And just because someone treats you a certain way doesn't mean that you have to act that certain way. And sometimes, kindness is the best medicine.

Talking about having to really adjust, when I came back to Pittsburgh after being in California for 37 years with a culture of tolerance and open thinking, I was going to come back here and share all of my skill and give back to where I was born and raised. I would sit down and cry and pray, asking God why I had come back into all of the racism. I just couldn't believe it.

When I went back to the University of Pittsburgh and worked in Institutional Advancement, I had all of my ties to Los Angeles and BET and we hosted a huge event up in Schenley Park. I had asked for a special office to have a marketing office but the University said no. With all the people I was connected with, I wanted to have an alumni reunion, we ended up shutting down the switchboard line. The operators called our department wanting to know what was going on. So they ended up having to give me a marketing department with separate phones and everything. And today, the 400 alumni of color I brought to that event with Diane Reeves.

I knew how to make those contacts so then the executive director of Institutional Advancement made sure I had what I needed, because she knew I was genuine and what I was doing was legitimate. We had all these LA entertainers here and it brought in money. More importantly, it brought in 400 alumni who are still connected to the University of Pittsburgh. I'm told all the time that when they have the African American Alumni Council homecoming dinner, that's who they send invitations to.

I brought back all the sports people who ran with Jesse Owens and Arnie Sowell, I brought all of them back together. I did a lot of things, because events were my thing and I knew how to do it and I feel like I have always had favor with it because it's a part of that service piece God has put in me. I have been here, worked hard and have been through a lot of negative situations, even here. For so long I was the only African American here [Arts Center} and there aren't that many still. When you trust God, He will move everybody and everything around when He wants you to be seen.

This is why we have to wait for Him and his timing. All that gave me much strength to encourage my children because when James was coming through all his training, he had scholarships to the best institutions that we could never have sent him to. I would tell him to go and stand up with dignity and integrity. He has always done that. Even Sarah said to me as she moved into stage managing in Sydney, Australia.

**JS: In case you aren't familiar with Hillsong, it is the foremost contemporary Christian worship company in the world based in Australia. I worked for another music company called Integrity Music and the Australians prayed because they wanted their own music. God heard their prayer and now they are planting churches all over the world. They have a huge church, one of the biggest in history, in London. Brian Houston is the lead pastor, some would call him the bishop. So when Joy talks about her granddaughter being involved with Hillsong, this is no small entity. It is a worldwide ministry that continues to produce tremendous music many of us would familiar with. It is quite an honor and most impressive that her grandchild would be connected.**

**KB: We have heard a lot of what has been going on in the present and past, but what are your plans for the future? I know you have a lot of them. Just give us the top one or two top plans you are looking at for the future.**

JoyS: I know I want to stay here until the Lord tells me to go, and that time is coming. I recently fell off a stage at an event and all. when I fell back, I don't know what made me turn except the Lord. I turned myself over and caught myself on my hands. If you look at me today, there is nothing wrong with them. I was blessed and God protected me, but it's time soon to make a transition.

I am involved in many other things, of course I am a supporter of youth ministries in Brazil, Uganda, Australia, and Iraq. I host an annual luncheon for the love and care family in Kampala, Uganda where James, Sarah, and Dara went several years ago. I want to continue to be connected with that because we solicit sponsors for Ugandan children. Those students can't come out of there unless they are graduating and want to come here for college. The first one we sponsored is almost finished. It's wonderful because she wants to go back [to Uganda]. I know I will continue to do that through church, because I can minister, contribute, and it's something for me to do.

I'm not one to sit down, because there is too much to be done. That's what I do even with my job. Some young couples want to come through and get married, and I'm with them for a year. I meet and talk with them and it gives me the opportunity to find out what they are doing and thinking. They always want me to sign their wedding books and they love me, and I always have a word for them. Hopefully I will continue to volunteer in major organizations. That's why I want to stay well because I need to stay well to serve others.

**JS: Is there a book in your future? You have some pretty interesting experiences and have come through several eras of American history, any thoughts of a book?**

JoyS: I have had many people ask me when I was going to write a book. I have seen myself with the book. I have seen it and had dreams about it. I don't know how it will come about. I'm sure I would have to be still or some situations to come. I would love to do that. And there are more ways now to do books and it's not so difficult. And I would love that. Because I would love to share my experiences with other women and Christians.

**JS: What is your favorite verse? I know you're a woman of the Word. Tell us about some of your favorite verses, books, or characters in the Bible.**

JoyS: I have some of the ones that all of us have. when I

say that, I speak of the one in Isaiah 54:17, "No weapon formed against me shall prosper." love that one. My very favorite is 2 Corinthians 5:21, "He who was made to know no sin that we might be made the righteousness of God in him." And of course the one I love to leave everyone with, I have several of them, Galatians 6:9, "Do not grow weary in well doing. For in due season, if you don't faint, you will reap what you sow." I love that advice about not fainting because we are living in times where it is the survival of the fittest. You really have to trust God and know who He is and know who you are if you are going to make it through these times.

The enemy is on a rampage and vicious. Our fight is not against flesh and blood, and it is so clear it is not, but against principalities and wickedness in high places. I rely on that word and find it coming out of my mouth all the time. Sometimes it is the way God has helped me apply and administer it and share it with people because many don't know it's a verse from Scripture. I do simple things like getting together with co-workers for lunch, and I will stop them and ask if we can say prayer. Or they will come and ask me for prayer. That's why I love God so much, because He shows us what to do. All we have to do is ask and trust and He does it and He does it over and over.

**KB: One of the things I want to point out is Joy is the best party planner and party giver I know. When you engage her to do something, you don't have to worry about it. It's done, she comes with ideas, everything is set up, and her people are so well trained. That's one of the things I wanted to thank Joy for. When she is looking for someone, we usually have a young person we can send her way. And what she does is get them into the word. She teaches them the soft skills of how to be on time and polite. She really provides a covering for them spiritually and also a mothering of them. So once you are one of Joy's peole, you never lose that wonderful relationship.**

JoyS: I appreciate that. My incentive to them, along with the things I try to provide for their heart and manners and culturally, is I am one of these people, and this is no braggadocio, I surprise them with some winter coat or some sneakers I hear them talking about, or even a cell phone. Something they can't get. I just tell them that I don't give away things unless they earn it. So they do. I have the best time with them and people come in asking me where I got them from. Because they are working in facilities where they are trying to transform and renew the minds of other young people. And they ask how I did it. I just tell them I am doing what I can do right where I am, as often as I can with everything I have in me. I know God hears me when I ask Him to help these boys and protect them. Because some of my boys don't come out of some fancy neighborhood, they come out of these hardcore neighborhoods. And I drive them back and take them if their parents come and get them. Because I don't want them to be on the street. But I want them to know that I care about them.

**KB: If a young person or someone who is interested in changing their occupation, retiring, or going back into the workforce, what advice would you give them?**

JoyS: Well, it depends on what they are doing. This business of retiring, it's not one of my favorite words, because I don't think we need to stop doing and being and giving. I have worked with people who have addictions while on the West Coast in this music business thing and I have seen the lives of people who are in Christian music, who have families, who are completely different people through Christ. And I made an effort to spend time with them to go back to the root. I believe we have to go back to our basic skills and look at what we have passion about, look at what you think you want to do and what you enjoyed doing in your life.

For example, I make an effort to spend time with people all the time. Thursdays are my "shingle day" when I hang my shingle on the door that "the doctor is in," because people come from everywhere all the time to talk to me. It would happen on the West Coast, too. I would move my chair and someone would go get it because they were coming into my office to talk to me about something personal. I go through it all the time. It's the way I start up talking with them about what they want to do. And I always want to find out what their spiritual foundation is. People tend to think about their mental ability, their physical and financial status and all of that. But they always want to leave that spiritual piece somewhere hanging off the side of the roof, as if it's religion, and that's not what it's about at all. I make an effort to deal with the whole person and find out what they have done and I always go back to those Scriptures about doing all things through Christ who strengthens you. My grandson has that verse tattooed on his chest.

I make an effort to tie people to some spiritual base and what it is they want to do, because this is how they are going to have to do things. God is not a magician, but he hears us. He has made us for something, and I make an effort to help them understand that piece. That there is a purpose for you that is good, that has value, that can be done. He will lead you and guide you to those assignments that will make you better than you ever thought you could be, to help you do the things you want to do.

URBAN HERO

# DR. LOLA THORPE

*Dr. Thorpe took over the leadership of her husband's church when he passed away a few years ago. In this candid and moving interview, Dr. Thorpe tells some of her story that has made her so prominent in Pittsburgh's church community. At at time in her life when she could have begun to shut down, Dr. Thorpe has increased her activity that caused her church not just to survive after her husband's passing, but to thrive. In this interview and her daughter Lisa's, you will read about women of courage in life and ministry who are worthy of the title, "Urban Heroes."*

**JS: Tell us a little about Dr. Lola Thorpe.**

LT: I am now the pastor of the North Side Institutional Church of God and Christ on the North Side of Pittsburgh, where my husband, who is now deceased, was originally the founder. We started this ministry in Pittsburgh in 1968 after moving from Philadelphia. I started with him as co-pastor throughout those years, upon which I retired from the Pittsburgh Board of Education and devoted my life to full-time ministry. And having served 40 years as co-pastor along with him, I began several ministries the Lord blessed me with. One was the inter-denominational prayer luncheon, the "So You're the Pastor's Wife Seminar," the We Do Married Group, the Women Out Working Conference.

The beginning of something great was the ministry the Lord led me to begin a Bible study on Wednesday evening. And I was with that for a couple years. I hosted also a radio program called *Moments of Inspiration* that was about eight years old and it was a daily program airing Monday through Friday. Then with PCTV I had the *Women in Ministry* there; sharing with women and discussing the importance of being used of God in ministry outside of the pulpit. So I am now the pastor with six adult children, 18 grandchildren, and five great-grandchildren, and working and helping to spread the Gospel, not only through Pittsburgh, but throughout the length and breadth of this country. In the early on years *When God Gave My Daughter Back* and it was published in the *Purpose Magazine* in 1997. My daughter had an aneurism at 28 years old and the Lord miraculously healed her and brought her back. So she is now working, alive, praising God, and just moved into ministry.

**JS: Talk about where you are from in Philly, growing up, and your family and the role they played in obviously a very productive and fruitful life in ministry.**

LT: My family was from an area called South Philadelphia, which my husband and I were from. We actually went to school together there. Then after marrying, we moved to a place called West Oak Lane. But my husband also pastored in an area called Camden, Delaware. We were there for about five years maybe. And it was such an experience and just a different vicinity and all for ministry. My daughter Lisa was born there in Delaware. In fact out of the six children, she was the only one not born in Philadelphia. And we moved from Delaware back to Philadelphia. So after purchasing our home there, after maybe eight months, my husband received a call to come to Pittsburgh.

Was that a challenge for me? Yes. Now I am leaving my family again, my mother and father. I'm the oldest of 14 children and my husband was evangelizing for many years. So we were packing up again and going to a place I knew not of. But for some reason, the Lord gave me the consolation that it was the call He had for my husband. So of course if it was for my husband, that meant it was for me. We rented our home out after eight months; it was our dream house at that time. I journeyed to Pittsburgh, leaving my mother and father and siblings behind. But with some assurance that it was the call of God on our lives, I felt very comfortable doing that.

Before we actually made the move, we commuted for eight months from Philadelphia to Pittsburgh, leaving Philadelphia at 4:30 in the morning and arriving around Sunday School time, then moving into Sunday morning service. Of course we had evening service at that time. And after that service we were back on the road, enroute back to Philadelphia. That was something that seemed unreal, now that I look back on it. It seems like an impossible move. We did that for eight months until the parsonage was ready here. And there was never a moment of distrust, unbelief or doubt of the fact that God might not be in it, because we sensed God. We journeyed on that road on 76 West every Sunday morning with six children; my baby was eight month olds. We took that trip to Pittsburgh, feeling it was the land God had called us to.

After the parsonage was prepared, we moved to Pittsburgh, and my husband continued pastoring here and went forward from that point on. The Lord blessed him. He purchased three buildings, as an act of faith, and he never had to go through the bank. God blessed him. My journey from Philadelphia to Pittsburgh was a trying one, but it was a glorious one. And on one trip to Pittsburgh, we came upon a tremendous storm and it was raining, thundering and lightning. The buses and trucks had pulled over and I asked my husband to stop. He said there was a service and he wanted to make the service. We were coming around a mountain and the Lord spoke into my spirit and said He wanted me to understand that if we could make it through the storm, the sun was going to shine. And we drove right out of that storm and into an area of sunshine. I truly recognized that it was the voice of the Lord that was speaking to me at that time.

**KB: Tell us a little bit about purchasing your church where you are now. I realize you have been through some things before you bought the church. Maybe you can fill us in on that.**

LT: On January 9, 2009, my husband was ill and paralyzed in a wheelchair. We were scheduled to have combined service with one of our partners in the city. The Lord sent a light snow and storm and we canceled the service. Around 7:00 that evening, we got a call that our church on California Avenue was on fire on. Upon arriving there, everything was in flames and it was gone. I had left someone with husband and told someone I had to go back to my husband and tell him all of his labor with the church was gone. He continued to ask if we got something out of the office. We tried to move forward to build and do several other things that did not work out.

I lost my husband on August 7, 2010. After that, I had a shoulder injury and went to have it repaired and my son kept saying, "Mom, I want you to come see a church." I needed to go to therapy and didn't want to and really didn't want to see a church at that point after 52 years of being married to a minister. But one afternoon, I had my son-in-law take me to the church at 302 West North Avenue, which was Holy Trinity Church at that time.

I went in wrapped up in a blanket wondering what I was doing there. I got inside of the building, and I heard the Spirit of the Lord speak to me to pursue this. I came home and called a board meeting at my home for Monday. And I assured them what I had seen and what the Lord had spoken to me. And I felt this was something God had set aside for us. We had the meeting and I spoke with them and talked and we agreed to have my son and go to speak with them and give them an offer and they accepted it. And from that moment, the wheels began to turn. God gave us favor with this ministry. They had the entire congregation come on and gave us a tour of the church. And I asked what about the banquet hall and the equipment. It seats 450 and has a commercial kitchen. They left us most of those things there. We agreed they would have the Greek festival in May and would continue to prepare the sanctuary for our dedication on June 18$^{th}$.

Of course we had the land on California Avenue that is still sitting there, but God moved on our behalf. It was miraculous, me being a single woman and not having to confront this before, always having my husband to go ahead of me. The favor of God was upon us. On April 5$^{th}$, God blessed us to close on that church. And they gave me the keys and I thought that I was just in another world. I put my husband's cross on and wanted to wear his chain. I felt so humbled within myself. On June 18$^{th}$ this year, I will celebrate four years having been there.

At some point, I was like, I want my husband here. I wanted him to see this. And my children were saying that this was what God was doing for me. And so, God has blessed us and I thank Him daily for what He has done. Because it is marvelous in my eyes and it is the Lord's doing. And God has given me my children to work with me there, and three of them are now in ministry. I am grateful to God for that.

**JS: Dr. Thorpe you have done a lot of things. You have been in ministry, media, written a book. Looking back, as an Urban Hero, talk to us about some of your most significant accomplishments. What do you look back on and say that was something, of all, the most special?**

LT: One of the things that was very special to me

was being able to air my radio ministry, *Moments of Inspiration*. It was called that because I had received inspiration from the Lord as to how I should send it out daily. One time one of my son's friends was murdered on the Hill.I began to pray for his mother over the radio. And as I began to pray for her, I included grandparents, mothers and aunts, all those who were raising children. A couple of mothers called me and wanted me after that to pray for someone specific. Out of that I declared a "Save the Children Day," and sister Gloria Briskey was on the radio at that time. Every day I would get response, and my heart went out to those parents and grandparents whose kids were walking the streets or on drugs, whatever it might be.

I took letters and received calls every day, and I declared a *Save the Children Day*, and I had two other sisters at the church who worked with me. And we put those names together and I came up with about 1,000 names. I said to the parents and those concerned, that on Saturday evening at midnight, we were going into the church, and we would take those names and I would lay hands on them and pray. We would neither eat nor drink. We remained in church from Saturday evening until the service closed on Sunday night. And I invited parents, if they desired, to bring those dear children past the church, so that along with my husband, we could anoint the children. It was so overwhelming, the parents and grandparents who came by the church, and then the calls we received. But we laid on the altar with those names all night long, praying for them. We were believing God for change in the lives of these young people. And so, when we finished that, we talked about it on the radio. It left such an impact with me, and God did miraculous things. I received testimonies from parents and grandparents, how God had done things in the lives of their children. That was one of the things from the radio ministry.

Then I began, since the Lord had blessed me to be able to put my children through school, the Lord blessed me to start the Lola M. Thorpe Scholarship, which for the past couple of years I have been able to share with children. And we had a committee and checked their classes. It had to be an accredited college they were going to. So we did that, up until now, every year for my birthday. It started because felt that I wanted to give back to someone. It was my birthday, so I figured whatever they gave me for my birthday I would use towards their scholarship.

And now I have young people who have gone on to receive their doctorates. I have a mother and daughter in my church who both received a scholarship. One year I had Jerome Bettis support me and had about eight schools that were represented. We went as far as Tuskeegee and Cheyney, all over, just sharing something. Not a lot, but just sharing something, to let them know that I wanted to encourage them to continue. Every year, it's a blessing when I see them graduate and have them come back to thank me. It's not all about that, it's just the fact you want to share and give to someone else, so that was another of my big things in ministry.

**KB: I hear you speak so highly of your husband. I wonder if there is anyone else who influenced you in your ministry in what you are doing today?**

LT: Yes, there was a lady, who is close to 90 years old now, in the city of Philadelphia. She brought a group of us young ladies together for a singing group. And we were called the "South Philadelphia Juniors." She gathered us up from the community and would bring us together at our rehearsal time and just loving to be with us and would teach us about Jesus. We became so attached to her, and if we had a spare afternoon or hour, we would go to Mrs. Lillian's house. She had a husband who was a minister, and her dad was actually our pastor. She was a woman who loved God and had great influence.

And one day, we were sitting on her steps, and she said, "I want you to know that Jesus loves you. And He can forgive you for anything you've ever done." And we were teenagers, and I was like, "Ohh, what is she talking about." And I left her house and we were all in a room and I was saying that I was going to get saved and give my life to Jesus. And they laughed at me, but those words never left me, over sixty years ago. I remember her saying that Jesus could forgive me. She and her husband started a prayer meeting in her home. Wisdom taught her to have it on a Saturday evening when most young people wanted to be out. We would go to her house for prayer meetings in her living room, and it was during one of those Saturday night meetings that the Lord came into my life.

I watched her in her marriage, and her home was like an open home. If the girls were there, the boys couldn't be, and if the boys were there, the girls couldn't be there, but she always wanted a home where people could come and feel free. We felt comfortable and loved by being there.

**JS: And it seems like you've tried to do the same thing. Correct me if I'm wrong, but young people and women seem to be a burden you have had throughout the course of your ministry. Would you say that's accurate?**

LT: Yes, absolutely. When I first came on the radio, I didn't realize there were a lot of women listening to me. One time I was on the radio and took my break after saying, "It's not your battle. You have no need to fight. It's not your battle." I received a letter in the mail from a young lady, who wrote that she was on the way to purchase a gun to take the life of a young man who she helped to get out of prison. Once she got him out, he turned on her and she said that she was going to get a gun and go kill him.

She was driving in her car and kept hearing me say that it wasn't her battle and that she had no need to fight. She wrote that she turned her car around after having almost gotten to the store and told God she would give it to Him. There are so many hurting people out there, that if they could just get a word of encouragement to let them know that there is a better way. If there is just someone who could reach them.

So yes. my burden is for women. And that was the theme of the Noble Women's Class I started. We got on the topic of healing damaged emotions and it was supposed to be a class lasting for maybe six months, but we ended up on that for two years. Within that session, God directed me to give each woman a band-aid. The Spirit of the Lord said to me to tell them if they could take that band-aid and put it on their scar or where they hurt, to do so now, knowing it was an inward pain and an inward scar, that only the Lord could heal. One girl took it and began to scream and holler, "I can, I can!" I was thinking, "Okay, Lord. I understand. This is my assignment for now."

**JS: Very good. Do you do the preaching in the church?**

LT: Yes. I like preaching, but I like talking, teaching and sharing with people. My husband was a tremendous preacher. I do okay, I guess. I like it, but I like touching people. I like to talk to them so they can take their mask soff. I did the "So You're the Pastor's Wife Seminar" all over this country for a while. I did it until my husband became ill because when I came along there was no one to speak to the pastor's wife. So I started this and moved it from city to city and just loved sharing with the women and talking to them. So, I do like preaching.

**JS: What have you been preaching on recently?**

LT: At present I'm recovering from a knee surgery, but before that I was dealing with the kingdom focused church, evangelism, and fellowship. I was sharing with the body about dealing and engaging in evangelism, which is enough to just stay on throughout the rest of the year. The importance of evangelizing In our area is so needed. I wanted people to feel confident that is what God is calling us to do, to go into the highways, to speak to people. We can't just be all in by ourselves. And so, I want them to feel empowered to do that and bring souls into the kingdom of God.

**KB: There is probably someone who is listening to what you are saying and thinking that the Lord is speaking to them. How would you suggest they prepare themselves for that task?**

LT: For the ministry? I would say that prayer and the word of God in studying to show thyself approved unto God. And of course if you are unto God, you are unto man. Then there is just prayer and seeking the face of God and interceding, sometimes not only for others, but yourself – for direction and for the leading of God.

**KB: What is your favorite Bible verse or verses?**

LT: Romans 8:28: "And we know that all things work together for the good of those who love him and have been called according to his purpose." Once, I began to cry out to God and grumble and complain, and God told me to read Romans 8:28. I kept saying that I knew it, but He told me to read it. When I got up and began to read the verse, the Lord said that I didn't know that it was working for me for good.

**JS: What do you do with down time? Do you have hobbies? What do you do to relax and stay fresh?**

LT: I read, I listen, and I do a lot of cheering with seniors. I have some young women who are incarcerated that I write. I'm a spiritual advisor for a couple of men; I write them words of encouragement. Then, of course, I have all my grandchildren. I go to their games. I had several grandchildren graduate this year, and I have two that came out of college and two going into college.

I went through a period of being very lonely without my husband because we did a lot of things together. So I share with my children and just people. I love people, and I love to encourage them – parents, mothers, wives. I find it edifying to talk to the young mothers about church, because that's so needed now.? So, I find things to occupy myself. I'm doing a little better now, but after 53 years of marriage and 13 brothers and sisters and six children of my own, being alone was not a nice feeling.

**JS: A life totally focused on ministry and other people.**

LT: Yes, I would say that. I have no desires now; there's nothing else for me to do. My heart grieves for mothers and I feel that we often speak of not having fathers in the home. But I feel like there has been a lack in the role of mothers. I think that mothers now need to step up. We're losing out children and don't have anyone to teach and share with them. Sometimes I get questions of how I kept my children and family together. Now they are all working with me in ministry. I'm asked how I did that and I say to love on them, share with them and encourage them. And, of course, Nathan, my grandson, went to Liberty yesterday to register for classes in August, and he came in and took his hat off and said, "Grandma, I'm getting ready to go." And he bowed his head and I knew he wanted me to anoint him in prayer. And I said, "The blessing of the Lord be with you and the favor of God go before you."

**JS: What are your future plans? What's left that you would still like to do? For your church, yourself, your family, media or ministry? Anything on the bucket list that you haven't checked off yet?**

LT: Well, last year I wrote an easy reader, *When the Worst Came First*, speaking about the hardships of marriage. And I took it from the perspective of marriage being for better or worst, and I told my story about how the worst came first. I published that last year. Right now I am thinking of writing something else, but I want to get more out into maybe shelters. I probably will do something on the Internet. I'm really seeking direction from the Lord as of what to do, because I know ministry for myself will not always be the same, and I want to be ready to shift when God says to shift. I still want to be used of Him. because I feel good for my age, having to deal with ministry. I want to be able to prepare people and empower them to be ready to take the baton and keep running. I believe the Lord is going to help me to do that.

One of my friends recently called me from Ohio and said the Lord told her to tell me my assignment is not yet finished. And I said, "You cannot be serious." But I took it very seriously, because I had been praying to the Lord. Therefore, I am waiting on direction, and I want to see a ministry that embraces all people who will come not only because of the name of the church or leaders, but because of the name of Jesus.

**KB: I was just thinking if you had advice for young mothers or a young girl who is pregnant with her first child. What kind of advice or preparation can you leave for her?**

LT: First of all, whatever the situation is and however you got into it – and I just experienced something like this in my very own family – that God is the giver of life. It doesn't matter where we are but it all adds up to where we are going. If she could just begin to understand that no matter state or condition or what she had done, that God is a God who forgives. He is a loving God and draws us, not only with love, but with kindness. He wants to be kind. He wants to show us a better way.

When we begin to seek him and accept His love, then that causes us to begin to love ourselves. Many people don't know how to love God because they don't know how to love themselves. Many young girls and young people in general are seeking love in the wrong places. If they can just understand, as Jeremiah said, that He loves us with an everlasting love. No matter what we do, or how or when we do it, He continues to love us. He's already paid the price. He has loved us enough to give His life for us.

I would say to them to say, "I want to have a new beginning. I want to start afresh and have another wind. I want my mind transformed and start thinking another way." They don't always have to be in the place they are in now. If they begin to search and seek out for things that are better and different, especially if they are preparing to bring a child into the world. If they have already brought a child into the world, then they need to think of things that are positive and not deal with things that are negative. It doesn't always have to be the way it is. They can do better. Maybe they don't have education, but they can go back to school. There are all different types of groups and programs that will help them, even with caring for their child while going to school. There is money, funds, grants, and things that can help them to better themselves. And when they better themselves, then that means they are making things better for their child. Of course when we see God and see Christ, He is the author and finisher of our faith. He causes all things to become new.

**JS: Good advice. You and your daughter are our first mother/daughter recipients of the Urban Hero award. And we're so delighted. Tell us about Lisa.**

LT: Lisa is my fifth child and a wonderful daughter. She is a daddy's girl. She loves the Lord and walks in a special anointing. She is the one, I believe, who God has allowed to come back from California, to bring calmness and spirituality among our children. She is gifted and is very smart. She's the baby girl and she is my daughter born while we were full-time in the ministry, and she is special. She walks under great anointing and I am very proud of her. Once we were on channel 21 together, mother/daughter, and she was sharing about growing up with two parents in ministry and the shifting and transition from my husband's ministry to mine. She explains that very well. She is a great mother and a great wife. Thank you all for considering me for the Urban Heroes program.

**KB: Absolutely. You and your daughter, individually, are two great candidates. It's a blessing to have both of you. Thank you for all you do for our community and the church family of Pittsburgh.**

URBAN HERO

## LISA THORPE-VAUGHN

*Lisa Thorpe-Vaughn is from a family with a fine spiritual pedigree and she is continuing the family tradition of excellence in ministry. Lisa's mother is also part of this year's Urban Heroes class, and they both provide a fascinating look into the world of family ministry. Lisa has carved out her own niche in ministry and tells us about her journey and her work in this high-energy interview.*

**JS: Tell us a little about yourself.**

LTV: Well, I'm multi-faceted. I love people, I love serving, and I love speaking and sharing information with people that helps them to grow. I believe I am called to those who serve others, so it's a huge leadership piece of who I am. I love seeing leaders grow as leaders or grow into leaders. That has been a passion of mine for years.

**KB: I first met you at Leadership Pittsburgh with John Stahl-Wert. How are you doing?**

LTV: I'm doing amazing. That was a great start for me there, initially as director of training for what is now called "Leadership Foundations of America." I put together annual national leadership trainings across the country. It was amazing seeing those things happen in different cities. Moving from there and when President Clinton was leaving office, being able to take 300 people into the first community-based initiative office of the White House. It was exciting and a great opportunity. That was the year we held our leadership training conference in D.C. It was exciting stuff on multiple levels.

The Leadership Foundation afforded me the ability to expand in leadership roles nationally. And then, I also took on the role of creating Amachi Pittsburgh, where we ministered to the children of prisoners and worked directly with Dr. Wilson Goode, in setting that up. I have worked with him ever since. I moved from the Pittsburgh Leadership Foundation into a national role with Dr. Goode recruiting and setting up all over the country recruiting the children, in most cases, directly through their parents who were incarcerated.

**KB: Let's start from the beginning again, with you. Tell us about yourself, your family, where you went to school.**

LTV: I am a "PK," since both of my parents have been in ministry all of my life. My father, who passed four years ago, was a bishop in the Church of God in Christ. I have served in ministry all of my life due to that, but it wasn't something forced on me. It was something my parents exemplified right in front of me, as they were serving people that came out of their love and passion for serving others. My mother has always been one who is extremely balanced. She was the oldest out of 16 kids. and she moved us out of Philadelphia, due to a lot of turmoil taking place in order for her to save my brothers from the drama that her younger brothers were going through. She just upped and decided to take us out of Philadelphia and take us to Pittsburgh. And my father started pastoring at that time here.

Two of her younger brothers had been murdered in the streets due to crime and all that was going on back then at the time. Thank goodness that she took the time with us. We commuted for a long time, back and forth, on the weekends, six kids and my parents. Then we all ended up together full-time on the North Side of Pittsburgh. We were there in the parsonage for three or four years, before my mother once again decided she wanted to pursue another area of life for all of us. She kind of got in my dad's ear a little bit and said she felt she needed to escalate the academic and educational piece for her kids. The best way she knew to do that was home ownership, so we moved out to Indiana Township and all six of us graduated from Fox Chapel High School.

I continued my education and graduated from the University of Pittsburgh for my undergrad. Then I received, for my community work, a scholarship from Carnegie Mellon University in order to pursue and complete my master's program in English in the cultural rhetoric. But it was solely based on the work I was doing in the community at that time, with the mentoring partnership of Southwestern Pennsylvania, which is a national organization. I started doing those workshops monthly for community groups. It just so happens that one of the individuals who attended one of the monthly workshops was Dr. Linda Flowers from CMU and we began to talk and communicate based about that. And it just went on from there.

**KB: Are you married?**

LTV: I have been married for 23 years as of April 20$^{th}$. My daughter just graduated from Syracuse University last month, and my son just graduated from Fox Chapel High School. He is headed now to the University of Arizona on an academic scholarship and to play football where he will be majoring in engineering. We have been blessed beyond measure. My husband is an elder with the Church of God in Christ, and he's my best friend and partner. I love him and he has been my greatest support outside of my parents. He is pushing my children and I through really being a man of God on every level. So I married my friend. And I still like him. How about that?

**JS: Tell us about the Leadership Training Institute.**

LTV: It's a non-profit organization I started in 2007. It

stemmed from the fact I was doing a lot of non-profit trainings around the city. Once I had decided to take the national position for recruiting for the national Amachi office, I created something that would allow me to not be limited to one organization. I knew that my calling was worldwide and not just to one church or organization, and it was to those who wanted to serve, primarily in a leadership capacity. And I started seeing the training piece as a launching pad for me to get into faith-based, community-based, school-based, and some work places.

And the creating of that organization also allowed me to gain access into the White House. Once I formalized it, I guess that was 2001 when I was honored at the White House, but my organization didn't formalize until 2007. after I had done a large mentoring workshop in Pittsburgh at our local church for everyone. People brought busloads in from Ohio and West Virginia and people drove from everywhere to be a part of this for 14 weeks. It was called Mentorship. One of our featured persons, Dr. Juanita Bynum, flew in every single Sunday night for 14 weeks to assist me with this mentoring piece for those who are in ministry. It just went on and on and on as I took and collated all the training I had been doing for years and brought it all together. We may have had more than 200 people who registered for that class.

We'd pack up and sit in line every Monday night, waiting to get into the building. And I thought, "Wow God, I feel good doing this. I feel like this is what you want me to do." However, once it was over, as with any calling or passion area, that's a lot of work. Immediately after that, I started a citywide 5am prayer I did for almost 12 years. So a lot of things went on top of each other to create a vehicle for me to do everything God has called me to do. I won't say I have multiple hats, but I pretty much synchronize my life where it's going. I look at it as one direction on the highway as you have other roads that will merge into the main road.

I know for a fact that I am a trainer and encourager of those who are in leadership. I know what I have been called to, and it was birthed from when I was a little girl. This was not something that just happened. I have always been connected to leaders. And it's given me a passion to want to grow leaders. And all of my life, everything has built up to that point. And that's what the nonprofit Leadership Training Institute meant to me. It was a way for me to bring everything under one umbrella and say, I do this, but I do that also. And I do 501(c)3's for those individuals and organizations that would like to legitimize their services and what they do and how they do it on a structured basis to receive funds. All of that along with the training has been my life.

One of the trainings I did that was featured at The White House was "Precision With Passion." A lot of people say passionate people aren't precise and are all over the place and you can't measure passion. I totally disagree with that. I believe there is a way to be passionate and structured with some precision. It can happen. Leadership and a structure to do that is what I like to assist others in doing so they can fulfill the call on their lives.

**JS: Looking back, what's the most significant accomplishment you have achieved in your very full life up to this point in time?**

LTV: There are three things and not just one. It's kind of a triangle. First is fulfilling the ministry God has called me to, in every aspect as I served with my parents and with people all of my life. We've had two churches burn down. I function very deeply in my local church. I believe that Christ created it as a tool to build the Kingdom. Being able to still do it passionately, love God and people after all I have been through is significant because a lot of preacher's kids and children end up bitter. And when they have an option to escape, they do. But God restored, renewed, and healed me from the inside out. And he renewed and restored my passion for ministry every single time we went through something that could have caused me to not love God and not love people. So number one is my staying consistent and committed to the call of ministry.

Second, I would have to say is my marriage. Being stable and staying in marriage is not easy. But God has graced me with a man of God who has been there and supported me in every single transition in my life, whether it as academic, our children, or whatever it was. I am proud to say I have been married as long as I have. Many said it couldn't be done. That is something I honor and respect and I am proud of.

Third, are my children. My son was a church drummer while the lead basketball player and an athletics scholar athlete all through high school. He has always been that. And my daughter is just graduating. I was listening to WORD FM one day, and one of the things someone said is you never know whether or not your children have accepted Christ into their life until they go away from home. When my daughter left for Syracuse, I didn't know if everything I taught her had actually stuck. But, thank God one of the first things she did was find a local church to attend. When she first went to that church, a few kids from that campus were attending. But by the time she left, they were doing van runs. They had purchased two vans and were picking up kids. She was passing the word. I was like, thank you, Lord, I just didn't know. Now with my son going off to college, I'm believing God for the same thing. He's been active in ministry as well, and they were never forced to be active in ministry. One of the things I taught them was how to pray and how to have a relationship with God. I believe there is a difference between church work and the work of the church. The work of the church is about soul winning. We can get caught up in church work, but then you understand the work of this church is a Kingdom principle in building the kingdom of God. It's about souls and witnessing and being who God has called you to be in a relationship to Him. That makes me happy.

**KB: As you are looking toward the future, looking back whose footsteps did you follow in?**

LTV: My mother. Years ago I probably would have said my mother and my father, but the older I get I am so my mother. I look at how I am raising my children, I look at myself even in my marriage, and I am so my mother. She pushed balance in life and that it's possible. A lot of people think you have to be all of this and none of this and all of that and none of this over here, but my mother has constantly taught balance. That balance has gotten me through all of these years of my life, marriage, and parenting. It's my mom. She's amazing. And she's still doing what she did and doing it at a pace I can't keep up with. I just have to work at it. She's still making it happen. When I look back on her ministry and the church burning down and my dad being sick for six years my mom took care of him and his desire was to always be at home. She never put him in a home and maintained ministry and caring for him for six years straight. He never missed a meal. When it was time for him to get dressed and go out, she made sure and presented him with the same dignity he had prior to his sickness. That's some kind of woman of God that she had some huge shoes to walk in. I stay close. I don't follow from afar. I follow close to her.

**JS: Mrs. Byrd mentioned the future. You're facing an empty nest, which is a big transition for you. What are the plans for the future for ministry or personally?**

LTV: Well I am in the process of writing a book. I have done ghost writing for years for a lot of famous people who have done very well. But after the last year, July 18th will be one year complete, and my goal is to finish this particular book which I am writing now, which will be my first "official book."I have done technical writing, but I've never done any writing outside of that, because that's my background. So, writing is one. I'm really excited about that and doing something for myself finally. And this book, for me, is doing something for myself, and presenting a portion of my life relationship-wise with myself and my daughter. But it's based on relationships in general between parents and children and how to grow that. And my goal now is to go back and get my doctorate degree.

**JS: What would you get your degree in?**

LTV: I am interested in creating a combination degree, with theology and political science. It's kind of like theology and politics, which is sort of controversial, but I think I have been graced for it. I am excited about putting it all together. I know there is a place for the kingdom of God in politics and our government. And I know it all wasn't developed off of faith, but it should continue that way. That we as believers should be somewhere in there making decisions, key decisions that affect our world. those of us who love God and are listening to God and are obedient to what God is saying about this world should be at the table. And my goal is to be one of the advocates for that.

**KB: And I think that's so needed. We are looking towards out communities and looking toward government to make changes, and we know that's just not going to work. I'm thinking of what you are doing is really needed for transformation of our world for the glory of God.**

LTV: Absolutely. And that's just how I am looking at

it. And I know it's like looking at the how-to-eat-an elephant analogy but I really am determined to do it one bite at a time. I am believing that God will position me at the right time in the right place so that lives will be saved. I've spent a lot of time in Africa and other parts of the world. I've gone all over spreading the gospel. My husband and I also have an international music group called Windburn. We take about 10-15 individuals out of the country in the month of November to January to do gospel concerts in Italy. We have done them in Stockholm. We've done it all over Italy and are working now to do it in China and areas like that.

He has done most of the work for that over the last six years. It's been an exciting ride getting the gospel out there however we can, in this case through music. A lot of times in Italy, they couldn't even understand what we were saying, but they felt it. They would ask, "At the end of each song, why do you say 'Hallelujah.'" Or, "How do you rock and clap at the same time while singing this music that we feel spirited about?" They don't even know how to explain it. But it's a tool and I am determined to use every single piece God has given me and equipped me with, to spread the gospel of Jesus Christ, that the kingdom of God might grow through some form of activity God has called me to.

**JS: Where have you been in Africa?**

LTV: I've been in Zambia, South Africa, Ghana, Kenya, Nigeria. I believe over the last year between 2013 and 2014 I had gone into Africa five times in one year. One of my clients was serving as an ambassador, so I was going in and out a lot with her, as well as she was speaking over different parts of Africa. We were working on setting up a hospital for her. We had a lot of business meetings as well as church services and conventions and conferences over there. So I have spent a lot of time in Africa traveling from one country to the next in 2013 and 2014. I have a few more countries to go over there, but I am good with what transpired. I was ready to come home. Most of them were short trips. The turnaround was quick, but they were 18 hour flights straight. And that was a lot. I wrote and got a lot of work done in preparation to do more work when I got there. So it was all Kingdom-based, Kingdom-purpose travel. It was good.

**JS: What do you to do stay fresh and recharge the batteries?**

LTV: I love to walk outside. I can't do a lot of the treadmill thing, but I love to just walk in the morning and breathe in fresh air. Something about that just renews me, strengthens me. I believe God speaks through so many different things that He has already created and I just allow it to refresh me. If He wants to talk, I listen. And if He doesn't want to talk and I just need to spend that quiet time with him walking and not asking him for anything, just enjoying his creation, that replenishes, restores and recharges me. After about 45 minutes of that, it's like, "Okay! Back to the wheel! Let's go! Let's make it happen." It's not always lights, camera, action, and a big idea when I am done, but I feel good.

I haven't always been this way and haven't always felt the way I feel right now. I'm in a new season in my life where I am excited about what is to come. I'm excited about my next, excited about my now, and I am open to the Spirit of God. I'm not going to ever box myself in again by titles or a position. I'm allowing God to have full reign in my life. I like not knowing what's going to be next. There's some level of refreshment and excitement that comes with that. It's like, "Hey, what's going on today, God? What are you saying? What are you doing? And what do you have for me to say and to do?" That's relaxing. Before, I held a lot of positions and did a lot of things. This season of life is different for me. This season really is Kingdom-minded and Kingdom-focused, and it's refreshing. I'm so out of the box.

**KB: You've energized me! Speaking of energy, what is your favorite Bible verse?**

LTV: Someone just asked me this the other day. I would say Luke 4:18. "The Spirit of the Lord is on me, because he has anointed me..." He has anointed me for Kingdom work and all those things that follow in that Scriptures. The Spirit of the Lord has anointed me. And I can't do what I do without that anointing.

**JS: Tell us about the church, when it meets, and where it is exactly and what services you have.**

LTV: We are located at 302 W. North Avenue, in the central area of the North Side. It's the former Greek Orthodox Church that they built across the street from Passavant Hospital. God has blessed us to be in that building. We are there Sunday mornings, Sunday school at 9:30, an 11 am worship service, Tuesday prayer at 6:30 pm and Bible studies from 7 pm until 8. We have one hour of prayer on the second Monday of the month. We are a church that has been built on prayer. We believe in that before we do anything else. We do have a lot of programs, but programs are not our drive. Prayer is the theme that builds our ministry.

We have a lot of special events going on. We have a banquet hall that is frequently rented out to community-based organizations and churches. It holds about 450 to 550 people banquet style and probably 750 theater style. We have events going on non-stop in that. God has graced us by giving us a sanctuary that is not only beautiful, blessed us with a facility that not only our ministry has access to, but the community at large has access to. And it's more than we've ever had. It's amazing, He blessed us during the recession to gain the greatest property that we have ever had.

**JS: And you alluded to it earlier, but what is your role in the church? What is it that you do?**

LTV: I am one of the associate ministers there and I am the servant leader for our Christian education department. I have done that for the past 12 years and leadership training is a big piece of what I do. My father's leadership and my mother's leadership styles are totally different, and always have been. I think that's why they worked so well together in ministry. But I have a large task, along with my CED team, in transitioning the entire ministry through, not just the leadership from my father to my mother, and how those styles really look, really training every single month, spending four or five hours really looking at the dynamic at how the ministry is changing.

Even the location has changed. We serve a different population of people, just because we are located in central North Side versus lower North Side, and keeping us abreast of who we're serving and how we're serving and how to be appropriate in what we are offering as service to our community and to each other. When I served at the Pittsburgh Leadership Foundation, I was a part of the transitioning from Reid Carpenter to Dr. John Stahl-Wert. It's ironic God had me on both levels at the same exact time, being smack in the middle of leadership transitions. And now I am actually doing workshops for organizations of faith on how you do a successful succession plan. What does that look like? How do you transition smoothly and shift gears? I call it the evacuation plan. Planning to move out and provide leadership for someone else and making sure they are ready, prepared and equipped for everything they need to be successful. That's my job at the church now, as well as being an associate minister, in support of my mom. I call her pomster; she's my mom and my pastor.

**JS: Any final words or words from advice for anyone who hears what you are doing and say that could never do that or accomplish that? What advice do you have as we close?**

**LTV: Stay connected. No man is an island. One of the first things the enemy tries to do is disconnect us from people who mean us well, who love us and support us. If he can get us disconnected, whether it's in job or marriage, or with our children - it doesn't matter. His goal is to divide. Stay connected to your local church, and not from afar. God is coming back for the church. People tend to look down on "church people", but I am a church person. I believe that Jesus called the church, and not man. It was in the mid of God, what we were supposed to do, as a local church. Stay connected and active. Keep loving on people and loving God. Love covers and love is persistent and love conquers.**

URBAN HERO

## MELISSA WHARTON

*We first met Melissa when she started her company that did some IT work for CUBM. Since then, we have stayed in touch and watched her grow along with her business. Today, she is a successful business woman in every sense of the word, and it was a pleasure getting caught up during to interview to hear where she has been, where she is and where she is going.*

**JS: Tell us a little bit about your business and give us an update on how the business is going and what you are learning.**

MW: I have a business called The Church Online. I am actually partners with Rev. Dr. William H. Curtis, who is the senior pastor over at Mt. Ararat Baptist Church, not too far from CUBM. I really enjoy what I do. It's not what I set out to do when I was growing up and through my childhood and through school. Through all of my, I guess you could say, life experiences, that's where it all pointed me to. And so, at The Church Online, we work with churches all over the country and some organizations internationally as well.

Our goal in what we do is to work with churches and nonprofits as well and help them with outreach strategies to grow their memberships and help them take advantage of technology so they understand that we are truly a visual society. We need to utilize all of the tools at our disposal to present our messages in a cohesive and professional way. And so, we do that through the development of websites, providing design services, and live and on-demand video streaming services, video production services, which is actually newer for us. We have also written several books for pastors all over the country by ghost writing. So, we keep ourselves busy with what we do every day.

**JS: I should say you do. How is business?**

MW: It's been going very well. We've been steadily growing over the last 13 years. And it's funny because one of the things I know to be true is that a lot of people don't really think about too much is there are more than 600,000 churches and obviously hundreds of thousands, if not millions, of nonprofits all over the world. And so we're in a very good niche, providing services that all those organizations need and use on a daily basis. We've continued to grow and enjoy that. I know we have worked with CUBM in the past and were very excited to have the opportunity to do that. It's been a great experience for us and we've continued to grow over the years.

**KB: Tell us a little bit about your background.**

MW: I have lived in Pittsburgh for most of my life. I have a twin sister, which a lot of people don't know. I was raised both by my mother and maternal grandmother, who passed away in 2007. Growing up, I spent a great deal of time focusing on sports and music. I played volleyball and played the piano and sang. I honestly had two goals. The first one was to be in the Olympics. The second was to become a Christian recording artist. So, I went off to college to Bucknell University to play volleyball and earn a bachelor's degree with a focus on voice and piano, which most people don't know.

When I graduated from Bucknell, I moved to Illinois for a short time and joined the US Dream Team for volleyball. And I learned a very valuable life lesson during that experience – we all have dreams and things we want to accomplish, but you have to be willing, number one, and able to really do what it takes to achieve those things.

Did I want to go on one day to be an Olympian? Yes. Did I enjoy being in a gym eight to ten hours a day, seven days a week? I hated that. After about six months of that, I returned home to Pittsburgh and never looked back to the goal of being an Olympian. At that point, I got a job at a transportation company that was working to bring high speed levitation trains to Pittsburgh. And I started working in their communications department, while at the same time, working as a minister of music at a local church. And it was really doing both of those experiences that I really discovered my passion for technology.

It's funny because a lot of people don't know, being the founder and the owner and president and CEO of what is basically a technology company, growing up and going through college, that I was afraid of technology. It's funny because when I was in college, for the longest time, I tried to avoid the computer lab like the plague, just because I didn't want to have anything to do with it. What I didn't realize was that sometimes your greatest fear when you take a hold of it head on can become one of your greatest strengths. And I think that's one of the things that happened with me, because it was during the time when I was working for the transportation company in communications and the director of music at this church, that I discovered my passion for technology and creativity, wanting to work with churches and nonprofits to help them improve everything they did to try to reach people. Because what I saw was that those two segments particularly had a tendency to put anything out because they didn't really have the knowledge or understanding, as well as the resources, of what to do. So that's something I really wanted to change and do. Fast forward fifteen years ago from that and I have grown a lot and really learned to position myself in the business in a place where we surround ourselves with the people who are experts in their field. So here I am today.

**KB: That is quite a story.**

**JS: Yes, it's quite a journey. Do you still play volleyball?**

MW: No, I have not touched a volleyball since I left Illinois.

**JS: Was church always a part of your world and life?**

MW: It was. It's interesting, I was always in church from when I was a baby. My mother and grandmother were very involved in activities in church, so we were always there. However, I was a person who always kept to myself. I was never involved in any major leadership activities at church, or any of those types of things that were going on. I decided at some point I wanted to be involved in working with churches, but I didn't understand what that fully entailed, until I actually started to work at a church once I graduated from college and came back from Illinois as well. I had always been a part of church and was saved when I was very young, probably when I was six or seven years old and have never truly left the church, so to speak, since then.

**KB: Tell me about your high school education.**

MW: I attended Penn Hills Senior High School, which was a good experience. You know it's something because we're doing the show, I guess, you're honoring people, so to speak, through this Urban Heroes initiative. But one thing I realized to be true through high school and even earlier, as educators, you never really know how you can influence the lives of your students. And I had a few teachers who really influenced my original path through school. I kind of kept to myself and focused on academics, music, and sports throughout my high school years.

**JS: Any challenges being a woman, having founded a company in an IT world that tends to be populated by men. Any challenges in that realm or lessons you have learned or things you have had to learn to overcome?**

MW: It's interesting because I think there have been a couple different challenges as far as that is concerned. Challenges it seems I experience are because of the mindsets of other people. And then there are challenges I have experienced because of a mindset I put on myself. As a woman, and as an African American, in technology, this particular area is dominated by males. So, a lot of times people just don't take me seriously, or they may believe I don't have much to offer. There have been cases when I was in a meeting somewhere, and I would be there with an employee who's male. If the people we're meeting with aren't familiar with our company and who we are, they just automatically assume that I work for my employee, not vice versa.

People form an opinion of me and the business before they really know what we are about, solely because of those two things: that I'm a woman and African American. But, that's the way our world works. It's something that doesn't really bother me, at this point. Now, when I would put certain criteria on myself it was funny, because when I first started the company, I thought being a woman and being an African American would be a hindrance to me. Even working with other organizations that were predominantly African American or women-owned. For years I didn't want anyone to know that I was actually African American because I had the mindset that, if they knew that, they would just keep going and not want to give us the time of day. I've realized that in many cases it's completely the opposite, and that's something I have worked through. To be honest, I now see it as a benefit because I am in a space doing something as a woman and an African American that most people aren't used to seeing. So, I've had a wakeup call, you could say, in understanding that it's a benefit to me and no longer something that is a hindrance.

**JS: So several times you mentioned paradigm shifts. A paradigm is just our world view or how we see things working and your shift when you decided you didn't want to make volleyball your whole life and how you see yourself in business. Have you found that your thinking is your greatest ally or greatest hindrance as you do business and relate to people? What have you learned in the area about the thought process and your thinking as an entrepreneur and a business woman.**

MW: As time has gone on, it has become my greatest asset. Over time, you're consistently and constantly learning, and learning to trust your judgment. I can't tell you all of the times I have had certain thought processes, second guessed myself, and then wished I hadn't done that later. But I've gotten to the point now where certain thought processes that I go through, and especially as an entrepreneur, I feel that it's very important that I have the ability to trust my judgment and those thought processes and be able to make those decisions I need to be able to make on a daily basis. That's something I do believe is very important in the day-to-day of what I do.

**KB: As an older African American woman who heads CUBM, I understand exactly what you are saying. I remember John and I had a visit from a banker once, and this person wouldn't talk to me. And John kept saying that I was the director, but the male refused to look at me. He looked at John the entire time. So I understand exactly what you are talking about. That's the blessing of knowing God. Because He can help us overcome anything we encounter. As we look at this, is there anyone you have patterned yourself after or a mentor you would like to share with us?**

MW: I wouldn't say I have any one specific mentor. But I will mention a few people. I'm just going to go back to athletics just for a moment. I feel that a lot of times some of those experiences you have in team sports and athletics can help to mold your thought process of how to work and achieve different things in life and not giving up on those things. Mr. Dan Brown, who was my junior high and high school volleyball coach, and a lot more than that in so many ways. He did a lot to help and mold certain areas of my life. He spent a lot of additional time working and helping me athletically and personally. So, he's someone I communicate with even still to this day.

And then, also Dr. Curtis who is my partner, who took a chance on partnering with and working with a young woman. When I approached him about The Church Online several years ago and had the wherewithal, God spoke to him and we've been working together ever since. He has a very good mind as it relates to what we do. A lot of people don't know, but he actually has a degree in programming. He used to be a programmer and a lot of people don't know that and he is very much into technology.

I would say also, my grandmother, who I mentioned passed away in 2007, helped raise me along with my mom. She was someone who had a profound impact on my life. A lot of people didn't know she was the victim of domestic violence for a number of years while she was raising my mother and her sister. She actually ended up in jail for a time, because she shot one of her husbands who was abusing her. But through all of that, her children and grandchildren were always the most important to her.

It's so funny when you think of a grandmother's love. There would be times when I was in college and any other situation afterwards where there would be, or could be certain things going on with me. You know how it is when you're in college, you're poor and broke when you're in school a lot of times and you wouldn't know what you are going to do. She would literally call me and say, "Melissa, what are you eating? Do you have any money?" She would send me little gifts and always making sure I was okay. Just being able to see the strength of her and being able to see the strength of my mom as a single mother raising two twin girls at the same time, on a low income, doing everything she could possibly do to make sure we had all the advantages we could have – piano lessons, dance lessons, and all the other types of activities we were involved in that she was working hard to pay for. But just seeing the sacrifices she made, which a lot of people see with their mothers and what they both went through is something that really helped to structure the person I am today, where I basically, and especially in business, always have a desire to keep moving, growing, and understanding that giving up, so to speak, is never an option. So I would say those are people who really had a profound impact on my life.

**JS: What do you do outside of work? Are you mentoring or training anyone? Are you still involved in music? What do you do to stay fresh? Hobbies? Talk to us about the Melissa in addition to the businesswoman and entrepreneur.**

MW: I have to be honest and say that I spend a lot of time with the business, really focusing on the success of that. It's not only what I do during the day, but it has, in a sense, also become my hobby because it's something I am consistently doing. One of the things that has become a passion of mine is working to help women, and people in general, understand that when they have a passion for something, if they want to start a business or ministry, that they can do it. That they don't have to have all the tools they need to do those things. They just have to be able to, number one, have a passion and skill set for the main thrust of it, but also understanding the importance of surrounding themselves with the tools, resources, and people that they need to get going. And to just really provide that support structure. That's something I have had a passion for over the years as well.

At the moment I don't do anything in an official capacity

at a church or elsewhere as it relates to music. But personally it is something I do in my spare time. I do still play the piano and sing. I do give some piano lessons to a few people that just have a desire to want to move forward in music. I am staying involved in those ways as well. I enjoy spending time with my family and just being able to have a little bit of time here and there to relax and enjoy my home and just life in general.

**KB: Where are your offices?**

MW: We are located in Forest Hills on Ardmore Blvd. There is an office complex up on a hill that is a group of red buildings. We are preparing within the next few weeks to take over an entire building in that complex.

**JS: Congratulations. Do you have a website and contact information for us?**

MW: The name of the company is The Church Online, LLC and the website is www.thechurchonline.com. If there is anyone interested in website development, graphic design services, live streaming video on-demand, video production, or book publishing services, they can contact us at that website and give us a call at 412.349.0049. And we also have a toll free number which is 1.866.794.9797. Through either phone or contacting us through our website, and even email at sales@thechurchonline.com, people can reach out to let us know what they need, if they have questions about what their desires are, we will do what we can to assist.

**KB: If you would, talk to people who are afraid of technology and the importance of being able to communicate with a younger generation and how this will enhance their professional and church life and just their life in general.**

MW: You know, there are two important things people need to realize. One, I think it can be a way out or easy to be afraid of something, because you have a fear of failing if you try to understand it. But you just have to take that step to try and understand those things. And it's very important now from a communication standpoint; if you look at probably the age group of between 18 to about 35, the way they communicate is completely different from the way people communicated just five or 10 years ago. And so it's of critical importance to be able to communicate with people in that age group in the ways they know how to communicate. We have more options and ways we communicate from social media to the Internet. And also, even in what we do with providing live video streaming and video services, a lot of people now are utilizing technologies like Roku devices, Netflix, Chromecast. Gone are the days of video tapes and cassettes.

It's funny because we'll get a lot of churches that tell us their CD and DVD sales are going down and they don't understand why. We ask how many of them actually own a CD player and no one owns one. You have to reach people where they are instead of trying to get people to purchase CDs and DVDs. They should be able to get online and watch or listen to a video. They should be able to download MP3s. They should be able to have access to different resources through iTunes. The proliferation of mobile devices, because of smart phones, is amazing. More traffic is generated through video and mobile devices than all other traffic on the internet. And that's because we have our smartphones and cellphones in our hands, literally, at all hours of the day. So we really need to be able to focus on utilizing technology, and especially with mobile devices to reach people.

So if you're a nonprofit, if you're a church, and you don't have a website that is mobile friendly, if you don't have a mobile app, then right from the beginning you don't have an opportunity to reach more than half of the people that are online at any given time. So that is another service we provide in building mobile apps. So that's something that's really key in being able to reach people where they really are. And if you don't really understand how to go about it in being able to partner with an organization or people or do is critical to anyone's success in being able to communicate in a way that's really going to reach the majority of people.

**JS: Unfortunately, as I had a pastor friend say, error is half way around the world before truth gets off the mark. And the church has been very slow to respond to technology. Do you find some have entrenched themselves and resisting and sort of proud of it? Do you find that attitude?**

MW: We do, but when we see that the churches are managed by people who are older who don't utilize the technology themselves and feel there is no value in it. And what you see happening with those churches is a certain demographic of people in their congregations and they are not growing. And they have a mindset of wanting to be able to do the same things in the same ways they always have done them, not understanding the value of trying to communicate in a different way.

On the flip side of that, we see churches that are managed by a younger demographic or who have younger people involved in their communications ministries who have been allowed to have more of a voice and role in the decisions of how things are done and how they try to reach out to people. And in almost every case that I have seen, those are the churches that are experiencing growth at a fast pace because they understand the importance of technology and some of these new ways to communicate.

A lot of people will look at the Internet and think, "Oh, that's the tool of the devil. Look at all these things that can happen with people using the Internet. That may be true, but there are also so many positive things that have happened from that. Just the possibility of being able to have a global reach, without needing to have a massive budget to be able to accomplish that, allows these churches and organizations to enlarge their territories in ways they would have never been able to do so before.

**JS: If they're interested in that. Because some aren't that interested. "It's us four and no more. And we're not that interested in reaching across the country." I'm intrigued; tell us about what kinds of books you have produced to help pastors?**

MW: We have a book publishing division at The Church Online and we provide ghost writing services. People would be surprised that a lot of pastors who write books have their area of expertise, which may not necessarily be writing a full length book with any type of professional literary excellence – without the knowledge they need to get to the finish line with their book. So many pastors are busy managing their churches, writing sermons, counseling, and those types of things, that they don't really have the time to focus on trying to produce a product that is marketable. We have a lot of pastors who come to us, either with a manuscript they have written and need it edited or that they started. They may come to us with sermon transcripts, a dissertation, or notes, and in some cases nothing at all and just with an idea, and they talk to us about what they want to accomplish. We put together a plan and our team actually puts together a full-bodied book for the pastor.

They are always a very integral part of the content development process because it's always our goal to make sure the pastor's thoughts, ideas, and points they are wanting to get across are always made in their voice. But we produce those books for them. This year, we have released seven books for pastors all over the country, and we have others that are in process now as we speak.

**KB: It's so exciting to see where you are now from when we**

**were last working together. And what I would like for you to speak to now are young people or people who would like to start their own business. What did you find was instrumental in keeping you focused and just as a little cheat sheet, if you could share with people that this is what you did and they can do it too?**

MW: If I am speaking to young people, I think there are some key things they need to understand and grab a hold of. One is that education is important. You have to care about and focus on learning, no matter what that may be, and understanding the importance of that. Education is something that no one can ever take away from you. The other thing is that a lot of people, when they want to accomplish things, want to see an amazing end result immediately. It is important to understand that nothing happens overnight. Things take time and you need to understand that you have to be committed to whatever your goal is. If you're looking at yourself now and thinking, "Well, this is where I want to be next year," you need to be looking at what are things going to look like ten years from now, and actually understand that you have to put yourself in a position where you can accomplish those things.

I know a lot of people who have wanted to accomplish things, but they have a family with responsibilities and things they have to handle. When you have those types of responsibilities, it can be a little bit more difficult to manage the growth and struggle that comes with trying to get to a certain place. They must really take advantage of the time when they are younger when they don't have the same type of responsibilities to really work towards building a career or getting an education or building a business.

Then understanding the value of surrounding yourself with the right people who are going to not only understand your vision, but be able to provide you with valuable feedback and support along the way. Those things are critical, because even though you may have a desire or dream to do something, every one of us needs that support structure in place to be able to keep going. Some of the most successful people in business understand that failure is a part of success. If you feel as though you've failed with something, but it's a goal and a dream you've had and truly want to see it through, understand that if you fail, you need to get back up and keep going. What is it you can do differently? What were the mistakes that were made? How can you move forward to do what you need to do? Understand that failing multiple times is a part of success.

**JS: Without giving away any proprietary secrets, what's on the bucket list? What are some of the next steps in the natural progression and growth of The Church Online?**

MW: We have actually worked with more than 2,000 churches and ministry leaders. We have completed more than 10,000 projects since we have been doing what we have been doing. One of the things we realize and have struggled with as a company is a lot of that work has been done for larger churches and organizations with budgets where they are able to take on and actually afford the expense of doing certain things. One of our goals that we do have in the pipeline is we want to be able to reach the smaller ministries, like churches with 75 members or people who have personal ministries that are trying to get started. Our goal is to allow those organizations to utilize our services. We have gotten so many phone calls and requests from smaller organizations in the past and they want to do things. Then when they understand the financial commitment involved, they're not able to move forward. We're currently in the process of putting together some systems that will allow us to be able to help them.

That's something that is exciting to us. And also to really understand the power of partnership with other denominations and organizations to allow them to be able to help the churches that are a part of their organizations with outreach by working with The Church Online. And so those are some of the major things that we have going in the pipeline also. And always, as a technology company, we are working to make sure we are staying in line with and at the forefront of technology, wanting to be able to ensure our customers and churches understand the importance of all those things and wanting to make them available to them as well.

**KB: It's really been a pleasure to talk and reconnect with you.**

MW: Thank you for allowing me to share. It's not every day that you have a chance to sit down and not only share, but just reflect personally yourself, on what you've come from and where you have gone to and where some of your goals have been. I do appreciate your giving me the opportunity to do that.

## The Center For Urban Biblical Ministry (CUBM)

Since 1988, CUBM has served the Pittsburgh area by training church leaders and members, offering accredited degrees in business, Christian ministry, and Human Services through Geneva College. More than 100 people have graduated and gone on to further education while serving with distinction in their local community and churches.

For information on how to pursue any of CUBM's degree programs or for information on the Urban Heroes Program, please use the contact information below.

The Center for Urban Biblical Ministry
7418 Penn Avenue
Pittsburgh, PA 15208

412.247.9010
www.cubm.org

www.ingramcontent.com/pod-product-compliance
Lightning Source LLC
LaVergne TN
LVHW051056080426
835508LV00019B/1906

* 9 7 8 1 6 3 3 6 0 0 2 0 1 *